Mix It Up!

16 Quilts from Cake Mix & Cupcake Mix Papers

Compiled by LISSA ALEXANDER

Moda All-Stars
Mix It Up! 16 Quilts from Cake Mix & Cupcake Mix Papers
© 2019 by Martingale®

Martingale®
19021 120th Ave. NE, Ste. 102
Bothell, WA 98011-9511 USA
ShopMartingale.com

Printed in China
24 23 22 21 20 19   8 7 6 5 4 3 2 1

Library of Congress Cataloging-in-Publication Data is available upon request.

ISBN: 978-1-68356-030-2

MISSION STATEMENT

We empower makers who use fabric and yarn to make life more enjoyable.

CREDITS

**PUBLISHER AND
CHIEF VISIONARY OFFICER**
Jennifer Erbe Keltner

CONTENT DIRECTOR
Karen Costello Soltys

DESIGN MANAGER
Adrienne Smitke

MANAGING EDITOR
Tina Cook

PRODUCTION MANAGER
Regina Girard

**ACQUISITIONS AND
DEVELOPMENT EDITOR**
Laurie Baker

**COVER AND
BOOK DESIGNER**
Kathy Kotomaimoce

TECHNICAL WRITER
Carolyn Beam

LOCATION PHOTOGRAPHER
Adam Albright

TECHNICAL EDITOR
Nancy Mahoney

STUDIO PHOTOGRAPHER
Brent Kane

COPY EDITOR
Melissa Bryan

ILLUSTRATOR
Sandy Loi

SPECIAL THANKS
Photography for this book was taken at the homes of Tracie Fish (Instagram: @fishtailcottage) of Bothell, Washington, and Libby Warnken of Ankeny, Iowa.

contents

just add fabric!

Do you wish there was an easier way to whip up a heaping helping of triangle-squares? Miss Rosie's Cake Mix and Cupcake Mix Recipe Cards to the rescue! What are they? A pack of preprinted paper sheets (called "Recipe Cards") meant to make sewing triangle-squares a cinch. Layer one 5" or 10" sheet atop two fabric squares that are right sides together and sew on the lines. It's that easy! Then slice the papers into perfect triangle-squares. No seam allowances to worry about. No tiny triangle points to feed underneath the presser foot. No stitching and flipping. Just quick-and-easy, perfectly pointed triangle-squares. We promise, it's that easy!

If sewing on paper is new to you, take a look at the tutorial starting on page 6 before you begin. If you can sew on a straight line, you've got this!

The Moda All-Stars have whipped up some delightful zero-calorie patterns for you! Sixteen designers picked a Miss Rosie's Cake Mix or Cupcake Mix Recipe Card pack and designed a quilt using them. Any quilt you make is sure to be a special treat. Each project specifies the Cake Mix or Cupcake Mix Recipe Card pack you'll need, the number of fabric squares required, plus yardage needed for background, borders, backing, and binding.

What you'll need:
- this book
- Recipe Card pack
- fabric

Find Cake Mix Recipe Card packs at your local quilt shop or online retailers. Be sure to buy the Recipe Number specified in the materials list for the pattern you wish to make; there are 12 options, and each one yields a different quantity and size of pieced units.

In keeping with our tradition, Moda is donating royalties for this book to Feeding America (FeedingAmerica.org). With your purchase, you're helping end hunger around the United States. Together, for every dollar we donate, we'll be helping provide as many as 10 meals for hungry children and adults. Now, that's sweet!

Thank you!

~ Lissa Alexander

Using Cake Mix and Cupcake Mix Recipe Papers

If you've never sewn with Cake Mix or Cupcake Mix recipe cards, you're in for a sweet treat! These foundation papers make it easy to make the best use of *all* the fabrics in a package of Layer Cake or charm pack squares. Sewing on the line makes your piecing and cutting precise, and the papers are easy to tear away when all the sewing and cutting is complete. If you're experienced with these papers, you can dive right in; if not, follow along below for the steps to success! The instructions call for Layer Cakes, but simply substitute charm squares if that's what you're using.

1 Place two Layer Cake squares right sides together with the lighter fabric on top. Center the recipe paper on top of the squares and pin to secure. Use enough pins so the layers won't shift. You can pin on the solid cutting lines, but keep pins clear from the broken lines—those are the stitching lines.

2 Shorten the stitch length to 12 to 14 stitches per inch—or a machine setting of 1.75 to 2. Thread your machine with 50-weight cotton thread.

3 Look for the starting point, which is marked with a star. Place the layers under your machine needle, put the needle down at the starting point, and stitch on the dotted lines following the turns and arrows. There's no need to stop and cut the thread when you get to the end of a line of stitching. Simply take a couple of stitches past the end of the line, lift the machine needle, turn the paper, and then begin again at the beginning of the next line for continuous stitching.

4 When you've stitched the last line, remove the unit from the machine. Take out the pins and check the underside to make sure that there are always two parallel lines of stitching, indicating that all the lines have been stitched. Check to make sure your stitching is neat and even and that you don't have skipped stitches or a thread nest on the bottom!

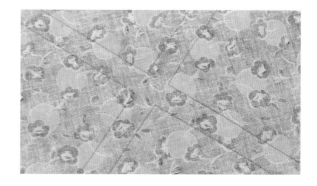

light on top

Why sew with the lighter fabric on top? That way you press the units open before removing the paper and the seams will automatically be pressed toward the darker fabric.

5 Place a stitched recipe paper on your cutting mat. Using a ruler and rotary cutter, cut exactly on the solid lines. Make the first long cut.

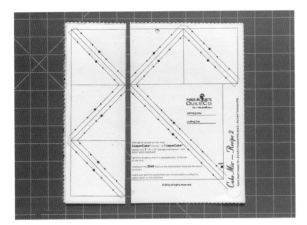

6 Separate the sections first, making the longest cuts you can before cutting apart individual units.

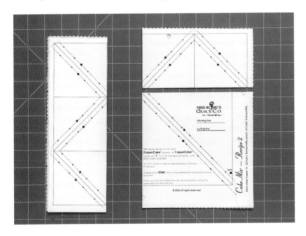

7 Move each section out of the way while trimming.

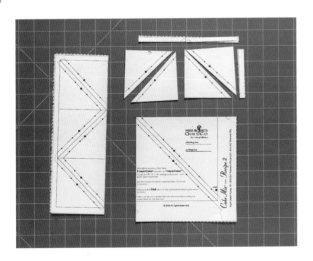

8 Make sure you've cut apart the pieces on all of the cutting lines.

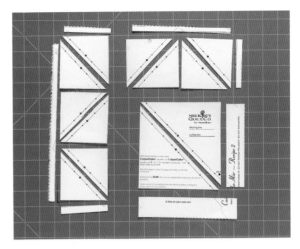

9 With the paper side down, press the dark triangle open; the seam allowances will be pressed toward the dark triangle. Press all the units.

10 To remove the papers, place your thumbnail on the seamline and bend the paper along the seamline to create a bit of a curve, and the paper will start to separate.

11 Keeping your thumbnail in place on the seam allowance, use your other hand to pull the paper triangle up and away. Then sweep your thumbnail back toward the seam allowance, removing the seam allowance strip of paper.

12 Trim "dog ears" from half-square triangles to reduce bulk at seam intersections.

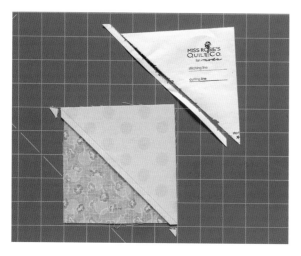

13 Lay out the units to make the blocks as instructed in the project you're making.

block options!

The projects in this book specify which Cake Mix or Cupcake Mix recipe cards to use and how to assemble the pieces to make the quilts shown. But notice on the front of the Cake Mix recipe pad that several block options are shown. Each recipe pad yields different sizes and quantities of half-square-triangle units—some include four patches, or a way to make hourglass units—but enough units to make the blocks shown. You can make any of the blocks with just two fabrics, or you can mix and match the units from other color combinations for lots of options!

bubble and froth

designed and pieced by CARRIE NELSON

Bigger is indeed better when it comes to this super-size Churn Dash. Contrast is the key to getting the block to pop off the solid gray background. But keep the sound turned down by choosing low-volume prints with minimal contrast for your assorted lights. The result is a quick-to-piece quilt that's big on style and super-easy to piece!

Finished quilt: **70½" × 70½"**
Finished block: **16" × 16"**

MATERIALS

Yardage is based on 42"-wide fabric and use of Cake Mix Recipe papers. Traditional cutting-method options can be found on page 95 but will require additional yardage.

▪ Cake Mix 4 (one pack)

38 squares, 10" × 10", of assorted light prints
     for blocks and inner border
3¼ yards of gray print for blocks and borders
⅝ yard of blue check for binding
4⅜ yards of fabric for backing
77" × 77" piece of batting

CUTTING

From the gray print, cut:

9 strips, 4½" × 42"; crosscut into:
   • 8 rectangles, 4½" × 16½"
   • 8 rectangles, 4½" × 12½"
   • 8 rectangles, 4½" × 8½"
   • 6 squares, 4½" × 4½"
4 strips, 8½" × 42"; crosscut into:
   • 4 strips, 8½" × 32½"
   • 2 squares, 4½" × 4½"
8 strips, 3½" × 42"

From the blue check, cut:

300" of 2¼"-wide bias strips

MAKING THE UNITS

This quilt uses Cake Mix 4, which yields eight half-square-triangle units, 4" × 4" finished, per recipe paper. (You'll need 19 papers.) Press the seam allowances as indicated by the arrows.

1 Organize the assorted print squares into pairs of nonmatching prints. Layer each pair, right sides together, with the lighter print on top. Use a highlighter to mark the section of the Cake Mix recipe paper you *won't* be sewing, as shown below. Then pin a recipe paper to the top of each

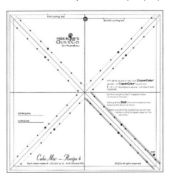

pair. Stitch on the dotted lines, making sure to stitch only three of the squares.

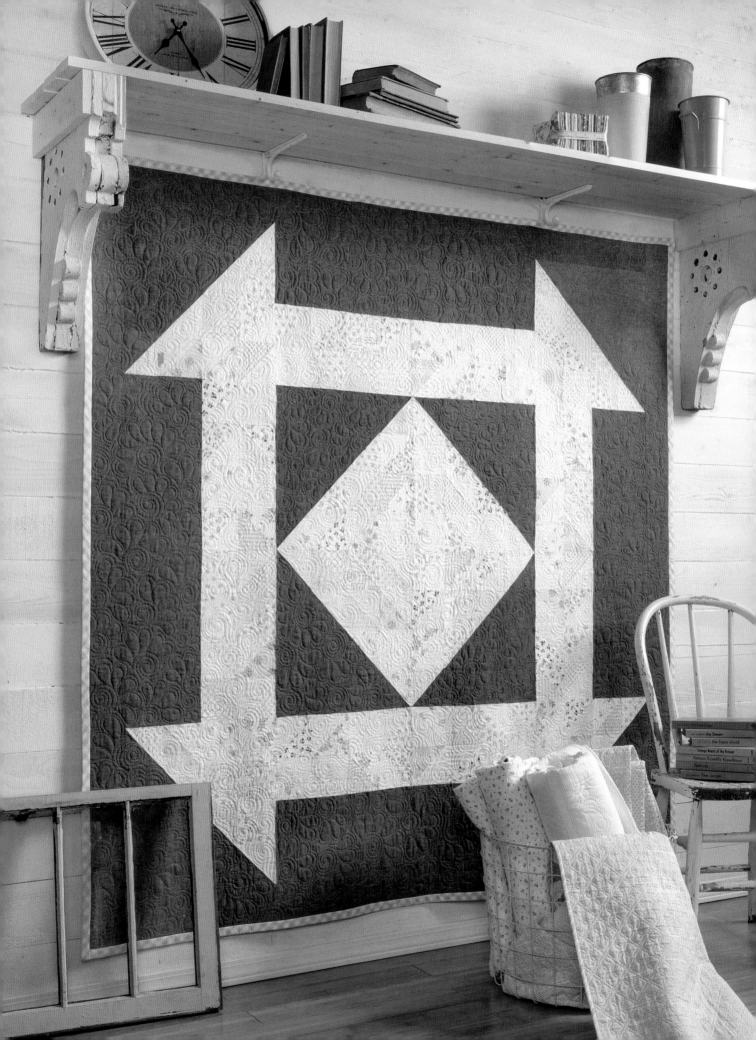

2 Cut apart the stitched squares on the solid lines, starting with the horizontal and vertical lines. Trim on the *outside* 4" line and then cut on the solid diagonal lines. Press and remove the papers to make six half-square-triangle units measuring 4½" square, including seam allowances. Make 114 units (2 will be left over.) Trim the squares to 4½" square, including seam allowances.

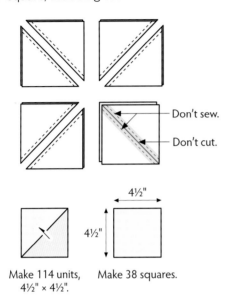

Don't sew.

Don't cut.

4½"

4½"

Make 114 units,
4½" × 4½".   Make 38 squares.

MAKING THE BLOCKS

1 Choose 32 of the 4½" print squares and draw a diagonal line from corner to corner on the wrong side of the squares. Place a marked square on one end of a gray 4½" × 16½" rectangle, right sides together and with the marked line oriented as shown. Sew on the marked line. Trim the excess corner fabric, ¼" from the stitched line. (To make use of your scraps, consider stitching a second line ½" below the first; trim between the lines and use the resulting half-square triangles in a pillow or table topper.) Make eight units measuring 4½" × 16½", including seam allowances.

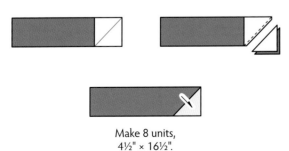

Make 8 units,
4½" × 16½".

2 Repeat step 1 to sew a marked square on one end of a gray 4½" × 12½" rectangle. Trim the excess corner fabric, ¼" from the stitched line. Make eight units measuring 4½" × 12½", including seam allowances.

Make 8 units,
4½" × 12½".

3 In the same way, sew a marked square on one end of a gray 4½" × 8½" rectangle. Trim the excess corner fabric, ¼" from the stitched line. Make eight units measuring 4½" × 8½", including seam allowances.

Make 8 units,
4½" × 8½".

4 Place a marked square on top of a gray square, right sides together. Sew on the marked line. Trim the excess corner fabric, ¼" from the stitched line. Make eight units measuring 4½" square, including seam allowances.

Make 8 units,
4½" × 4½".

Quilted by Carrie Straka of Red Velvet Quilting

Don't be afraid to choose light prints with a variety of colors in them. In small scale, the bits of color add interest without attracting too much attention.

5 Lay out the units from steps 1–4 and six different half-square-triangle units in four rows as shown. Sew the units together into rows. Join the rows to make a block measuring 16½" square, including seam allowances. Make eight blocks.

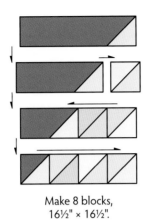

Make 8 blocks,
16½" × 16½".

MAKING THE BORDER UNITS

1 Lay out 16 half-square-triangle units in two rows, making sure to orient the units as shown. Sew the units together into rows. Join the rows to make a pieced strip measuring 8½" × 32½", including seam allowances. Make four units.

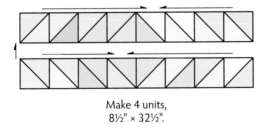

Make 4 units,
8½" × 32½".

2 Sew a gray 8½" × 32½" strip to one long edge of a pieced strip to make a border unit measuring 16½" × 32½", including seam allowances. Make four units.

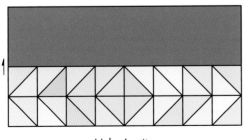

Make 4 units,
16½" × 32½".

ASSEMBLING THE QUILT TOP

1 Lay out the blocks and border units as shown in the quilt assembly diagram below. Sew the center blocks together to make a large block measuring 32½" square, including seam allowances.

2 Sew the blocks and border units together into rows. Join the rows to make the quilt-top center. The quilt top should measure 64½" square, including seam allowances.

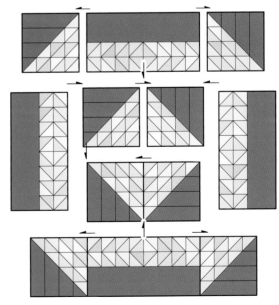

Quilt assembly

Secret Ingredients

from Carrie Nelson

Read all about it! Cake Mix and Cupcake Mix papers have Carrie Nelson's name written all over them—literally, they carry the Miss Rosie's Quilt Co. for Moda brand on every pack. She's the brains behind these beauties!

Three ingredients I have to have at the ready when I'm sewing are water (preferably sparkling), an audiobook or music, and at least twice as much fabric as I need for the project. I like having options because . . . scrappy.

My favorite mix of colors almost always includes red and green. And whenever possible, orange, yellow, purple, and gray.

When a quilt design needs a little something extra, I love to mix in fabric from several different collections. And stripes and polka dots too.

One of the best mixes I buy is the Divina Greek Olives Mix from Central Market.

If I made a mix tape, the artist whose music would be on it for sure is Ed Sheeran.

When it comes to mixing it up in the kitchen, two unlikely things I like mixed together are fresh goat cheese infused with lavender. It's a store-bought cheese, Purple Haze by Cypress Grove.

In a bowl of snack mix, my favorite is anything that looks and tastes like a cracker, **and my least favorites are** the pretzels and anything sweet, such as M&M's or candy.

The most common mix-up I make when sewing is I sometimes forget to lengthen the stitch length after stitching all of my Cake Mix recipe papers with shorter stitches.

3 Join two gray 3½"-wide strips end to end to make a border strip. Make four strips. Trim two strips to 64½" long and sew them to opposite sides of the quilt top. Trim the remaining two strips to 70½" long and sew them to the top and bottom of the quilt top, which should measure 70½" square.

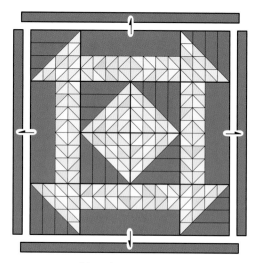

Adding the outer borders

FINISHING THE QUILT

For help with any of the finishing steps, including bias binding, go to ShopMartingale.com/HowtoQuilt for free downloadable information.

1 Layer the quilt top, batting, and backing; baste.

2 Quilt by hand or machine. The quilt shown is machine quilted with an allover design of loops and swirls.

3 Use the blue check 2¼"-wide bias strips to make the binding, and then attach the binding to the quilt. (Note that the quilt on page 12 features a wider than usual binding. It was made with a 3½"-wide single-fold bias strip that finished to ¾" wide.)

hot cross buns

designed and pieced by SUSAN ACHE

We're positive you'll get a kick out of choosing your fabric combinations for this colorful throw. With the help of Cake Mix 3, you simply pair two 10" squares from your stack and sew. Choose a third fabric for the plus sign in the block center. Add some scrappy, low-volume sashing and it all adds up to one fabulously scrappy quilt!

Finished quilt: **78½" × 78½"**
Finished block: **10" × 10"**

MATERIALS

Yardage is based on 42"-wide fabric and use of Cake Mix Recipe papers. Traditional cutting-method options can be found on page 95 but will require additional yardage.

▨ Cake Mix 3 (one pack)

⅓ yard *each* of 12 assorted light prints for blocks
54 squares, 10" × 10", of assorted medium or dark prints for blocks and sashing (referred to collectively as "dark")
25 squares, 10" × 10", of assorted light prints for sashing
1⅞ yards of cream dot for sashing, border, and binding
7¼ yards of fabric for backing
87" × 87" piece of batting

CUTTING

From *each* of the 12 assorted light prints for blocks, cut:

1 strip, 10" × 42"; crosscut into 4 squares, 10" × 10" (48 total). Crosscut *1 square of each color* into 12 squares, 2½" × 2½" (144 total).

From *each* of 18 dark squares, cut:

3 strips, 2½" × 10"; crosscut into:
  • 2 rectangles, 2½" × 6½" (36 total)
  • 4 squares, 2½" × 2½" (72 total)
  • 3 squares, 1½" × 1½" (54 total)
1 strip, 1½" × 10"; crosscut into 5 squares, 1½" × 1½" (90 total)

From *each* of 20 light squares for sashing, cut:

3 strips, 2½" × 10"; crosscut into 5 rectangles, 2½" × 4½" (100 total)
1 strip, 1½" × 10"; crosscut into 2 rectangles, 1½" × 4½" (40 total)

From *each* of 4 light squares for sashing, cut:

2 strips, 2½" × 10"; crosscut into 4 rectangles, 2½" × 4½" (16 total)
1 strip, 1½" × 10"; crosscut into 2 rectangles, 1½" × 4½" (8 total)

From the 1 remaining light square for sashing, cut:

2 strips, 2½" × 10"; crosscut into 4 rectangles, 2½" × 4½"

From the cream dot, cut:

4 strips, 2½" × 42"; crosscut into 60 squares, 2½" × 2½"
2 strips, 1½" × 42"; crosscut into 24 rectangles, 1½" × 2½"
8 strips, 3½" × 42"
9 strips, 2¼" × 42"

MAKING THE UNITS

This quilt uses Cake Mix 3, which yields 18 half-square-triangle units, 2" × 2" finished, per recipe paper. (You'll need 36 papers.) Press the seam allowances as indicated by the arrows.

1 Pair a light 10" square with a dark 10" square, right sides together with the light square on top. Pin a Cake Mix recipe paper to the top of each pair. Stitch on the dotted lines as indicated on the paper. Sew 36 pairs.

2 Cut apart the stitched squares on the solid lines, starting with the horizontal and vertical lines. Press and remove the papers to make 18 half-square-triangle units measuring 2½" square, including seam allowances. Make 648 units.

Make 648 units,
2½" × 2½".

MAKING THE BLOCKS

For each block, you'll need 16 matching half-square-triangle units and four light 2½" squares, all with matching backgrounds. You'll also need two dark 2½" squares and one dark 2½" × 6½" rectangle, all matching. You'll have a total of 72 half-square-triangle units left over for another project.

1 Lay out the half-square-triangle units in two rows of two, noting the orientation of the units. Sew the units together into rows. Join the rows to make a corner unit measuring 4½" square, including seam allowances. Make four units.

Make 4 units,
4½" × 4½".

2 Join one light square and one dark 2½" square to make a two-patch unit measuring 2½" × 4½", including seam allowances. Make two units.

Make 2 units,
2½" × 4½".

3 Join two light 2½" squares and one dark rectangle to make a center unit measuring 2½" × 10½", including seam allowances.

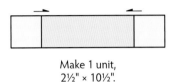

Make 1 unit,
2½" × 10½".

4 Lay out the corner units, two-patch units, and center unit in three columns. Sew the corner units and two-patch units together into columns. Join the columns to the center unit to make a block measuring 10½" square, including seam allowances. Make 36 blocks.

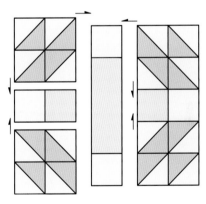

Make 36 blocks,
10½" × 10½".

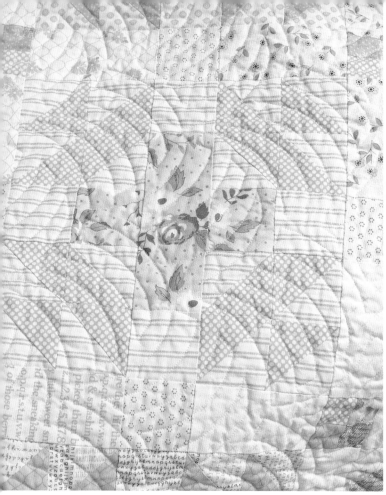

MAKING THE SASHING UNITS

Refer to the photo on page 19 and the quilt assembly diagram on page 20 as needed for placement guidance.

1. Lay out four assorted dark 1½" squares in two rows of two. Sew the squares together into rows. Join the rows to make a four-patch unit measuring 2½" square, including seam allowances. Make 25 four-patch units.

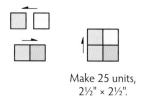

Make 25 units,
2½" × 2½".

2. Join two assorted dark 1½" squares to make a two-patch unit measuring 1½" × 2½", including seam allowances. Make 20 two-patch units.

Make 20 units,
2½" × 2½".

3. On a design wall, lay out the blocks in six rows of six blocks each, referring to the quilt assembly diagram on page 20. Place a four-patch unit at each block intersection. Position four matching light 2½" × 4½" rectangles around each four-patch unit.

4. Around the perimeter of the blocks, place a two-patch unit at each block intersection and a dark 1½" square in each corner. Position two light 1½" × 4½" rectangles and one light 2½" × 4½"

Quilted by Susan Rogers

A lagniappe is something given gratuitously or by way of good measure. The four-patch sashing cornerstones are the lagniappe or little something extra here.

rectangle, all matching, around each two-patch unit. Place matching light 1½" × 4½" rectangles on adjacent sides of each corner square.

5 Pin a cream 2½" square between the light 2½" × 4½" rectangles. Pin a cream 1½" × 2½" rectangle between the light 1½" × 4½" rectangles around the perimeter.

6 Sew two light 2½" × 4½" rectangles and a cream 2½" square together to make a sashing unit measuring 2½" × 10½", including seam allowances. Return the unit to its correct position on the design wall. Make 60 units.

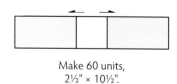

Make 60 units,
2½" × 10½".

7 Sew two light 1½" × 4½" rectangles and a cream 1½" × 2½" rectangle together to make a sashing unit measuring 1½" × 10½", including seam allowances. Return the unit to its correct position on the design wall. Make 24 units.

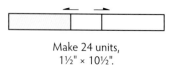

Make 24 units,
1½" × 10½".

ASSEMBLING THE QUILT TOP

1 Sew the pieces together into rows, keeping the rows in the correct order on the design wall. Join the rows to complete the quilt-top center. The quilt top should measure 72½" square, including seam allowances.

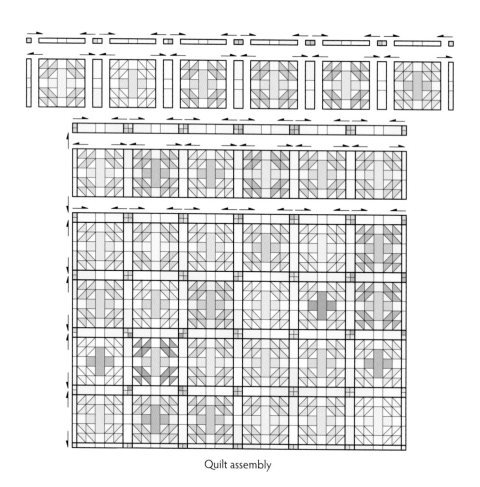

Quilt assembly

2 Join the cream dot 3½"-wide strips end to end in pairs. Trim two of the pieced strips to 78½" long and trim two strips to 72½" long. Sew the shorter strips to opposite sides of the quilt top. Sew the longer strips to the top and bottom of the quilt top. The quilt top should measure 78½" square.

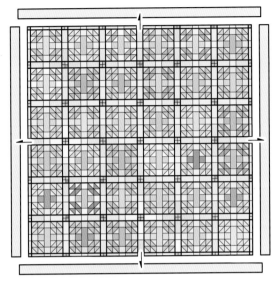

Adding the borders

FINISHING THE QUILT

For help with any of the finishing steps, go to ShopMartingale.com/HowtoQuilt for free downloadable information.

1 Layer the quilt top, batting, and backing; baste.

2 Quilt by hand or machine. The quilt shown is machine quilted with a Baptist Fan design.

3 Use the cream dot 2¼"-wide strips to make the binding, and then attach the binding to the quilt.

Secret Ingredients

from Susan Ache

Remember the social mixers of the '70s and '80s? Well, we'd all be wishing Susan Ache was at our party—then and now. She's a ton of fun! Catch up with her wit and wisdom on Instagram (@yardgrl60).

Three ingredients I have to have at the ready when I'm sewing are (1) all my fabrics folded, (2) stacked by color, and (3) ready to be cut in order.

My favorite mix of colors almost always includes red and orange.

When a quilt design needs a little something extra, I mix in a fun fabric shape from a cool template or tool.

One of the best mixes I buy is queso mix.

If I made a mix tape, the artist whose music would be on it for sure is Bruno Mars.

When it comes to mixing it up in the kitchen, two unlikely things I like to mix together are popcorn and Milk Duds.

Two things others like to mix—but I don't—are navy and brown, or pineapple and strawberries together on a fruit plate.

In a bowl of snack mix, my favorites are the M&M's and melba rounds, **and my least favorites** (ugh) are the pretzels and peanut-butter nuggets.

The most common mix-up I make when sewing is turning my half-square triangles the wrong direction in a block.

Stand mixer or hand mixer? Stand mixer (a KitchenAid).

all my Ts

designed by BRIGITTE HEITLAND

If your favorite color is rainbow, here's a quilt that will be oh-so-popular. The playful arrangement of colorful T blocks couldn't be more fun. Beginning with a Cake Mix, stitching the half-square triangles for the tees is a breeze. On your mark, get set, sew!

Finished quilt: **61¼" × 61¼"**
Finished block: **6¾" × 6¾"**

MATERIALS

Yardage is based on 42"-wide fabric and use of Cake Mix Recipe papers. Traditional cutting-method options can be found on page 95 but will require additional yardage.

 Cake Mix 2 (one pack)

41 squares, 10" × 10", of assorted prints for blocks
3⅜ yards of light gray solid for blocks
½ yard of dark gray print for binding
3⅞ yards of fabric for backing
68" × 68" piece of batting

CUTTING

From the light gray solid, cut:
11 strips, 10" × 42"; crosscut into 41 squares,
    10" × 10"

From the dark gray print, cut:
7 strips, 2¼" × 42"

MAKING THE UNITS

This quilt uses Cake Mix 2, which yields 10 half-square-triangle units, 2¼" × 2¼" finished, and two half-square-triangle units, 4½" × 4½" finished, per recipe paper. (You'll need 41 papers.) Press the seam allowances as indicated by the arrows.

1 Pair each print square with a light gray square, right sides together with the light gray square on top. Pin a Cake Mix recipe paper to the top of each pair. Stitch on the dotted lines as indicated on the paper.

2 Cut apart the stitched squares on the solid lines. Press and remove the papers to make 10 A units measuring 2¾" square, including seam allowances, and two B units measuring 5" square, including seam allowances. Make 410 of unit A and 82 of unit B.

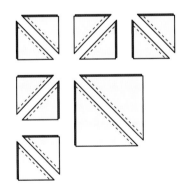

Unit A.
Make 410 units,
2¾" × 2¾".

Unit B.
Make 82 units,
5" × 5".

Pieced by Sarah Huechteman;
quilted by Carrie Straka of Red Velvet Quilting

MAKING THE BLOCKS

Each block uses five A units and one B unit, all matching.

1 Join two matching A units, making sure to orient the units as shown. Make 81 units measuring 2¾" × 5", including seam allowances. Reverse the orientation of the A units to make 81 reversed units.

Make 81 of each unit,
2¾" × 5".

2 Lay out one of each unit from step 1, the remaining A unit, and the B unit (all matching) in two rows. Sew the units together into rows. Join the rows to make a block measuring 7¼" square, including seam allowances. Make 81 blocks. You'll have five A units and one B unit left over for another project.

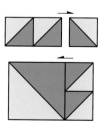 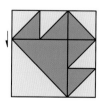

Make 81 blocks,
7¼" × 7¼".

ASSEMBLING THE QUILT TOP

Lay out the blocks in nine rows of nine blocks each. For inspiration, refer to the photo on page 24 to see how the blocks in the featured quilt form a gradation of colors. Sew the blocks together into rows. Join the rows to complete the quilt top. The quilt top should measure 61¼" square.

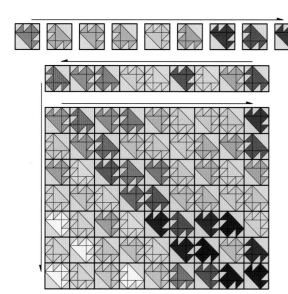

Quilt assembly

FINISHING THE QUILT

For help with any of the finishing steps, go to ShopMartingale.com/HowtoQuilt for free downloadable information.

1 Layer the quilt top, batting, and backing; baste.

2 Quilt by hand or machine. The quilt shown is machine quilted with an allover swirl design.

3 Use the dark gray 2¼"-wide strips to make the binding, and then attach the binding to the quilt.

Secret Ingredients

from Brigitte Heitland

She's chic, alright! Zen Chic, that is. Brigitte Heitland (BrigitteHeitland.de) is an interior designer by training, so she's all about creating eye-catching quilts. We've got our eye on you, Brigitte!

Three ingredients I have to have at the ready when I'm sewing are my iron for lots of steaming, an extra light source next to my sewing machine, and an audiobook.

My favorite mix of colors almost always includes my special Bella Solid Zen Grey.

When a quilt design needs a little something extra, I love to mix in asymmetry.

One of the best mixes I buy is a cereal mix with different single-serve flavors.

If I made a mix tape, the artist whose music would be on it for sure is Sting, with the song "Whenever I Say Your Name."

When it comes to mixing it up in the kitchen, unlikely things I like to mix together are garlic, lemon, and honey. Try it on grilled salmon . . . yummy!

In a bowl of snack mix, my favorites are the peanuts, **and my least favorite is** the Chex cereal.

The most common mix-up I make when sewing is when I'm paper piecing. I sometimes position the piece incorrectly so that when it's flipped it doesn't cover the segment that it should.

Stand mixer or hand mixer? Both, since you can never *mix* enough!

pin me

designed by LYNNE HAGMEIER

Spin your pinwheels 'round and 'round, you'll be ready to go to town with this Cupcake Mix cutie. Whether you make it for use as a wall hanging or a turn it into a table runner, the pattern is perfect to showcase 5" charm squares.

Finished quilt: **22½" × 37½"**
Finished block: **6" × 6"**

MATERIALS

Yardage is based on 42"-wide fabric and use of Cake Mix Recipe papers. Traditional cutting-method options can be found on page 95 but will require additional yardage.

 **Cupcake Mix 2** (one pack)

28 squares, 5" × 5", of dark prints for blocks
  and inner border
½ yard of beige print for blocks
⅝ yard of tan floral for blocks and borders
⅓ yard of red tone on tone for binding
1¼ yards of fabric for backing
27" × 42" piece of batting

CUTTING

From the beige print, cut:

3 strips, 5" × 42"; crosscut into 21 squares, 5" × 5"

From the tan floral, cut:

1 strip, 5" × 42"; crosscut into 7 squares, 5" × 5"
2 strips, 2" × 42"; crosscut into:
  • 14 rectangles, 2" × 3½"
  • 2 rectangles, 2" × 6½"
  • 4 squares, 2" × 2"
4 strips, 2½" × 42"; crosscut into:
  • 2 strips, 2½" × 33½"
  • 2 strips, 2½" × 22½"

From the red tone on tone, cut:

4 strips, 2¼" × 42"

scrap it up

To achieve a scrappy look and have more options when positioning the half-square-triangle units, cut 14 of the recipe cards in half to create 28 rectangles, 2½" × 5". Each half will yield four half-square-triangle units. Cut seven beige squares, seven tan squares, and 14 dark squares in half. Sew and trim the same way as for the full Cupcake Mix recipe cards.

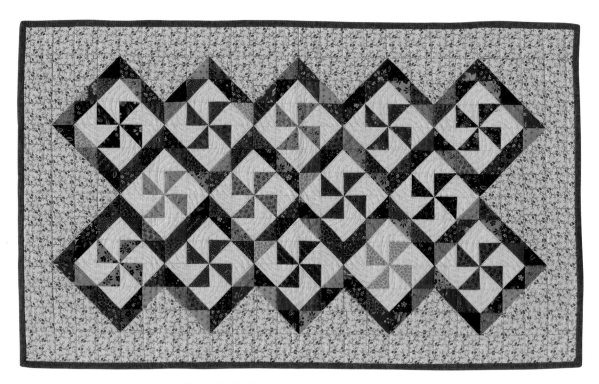

Pieced by Kathy Limpic; quilted by Joy Johnson

*Add or subtract a few pinwheels to customize the design to fit
your table or space in which the quilt will be displayed.*

MAKING THE UNITS

This quilt uses Cupcake Mix 2, which yields eight
half-square-triangle units, 1½" × 1½" finished, per
recipe paper. (You'll need 28 papers.) Press the seam
allowances as indicated by the arrows.

1 Place each beige square on top of a dark square,
right sides together. Pin a Cupcake Mix recipe
paper to the top of each pair. Stitch on the dotted
lines as indicated on the paper.

2 Cut apart the stitched squares on the solid lines,
starting with the horizontal and vertical lines. Trim
on the outside 4¾" line and then cut on the solid
diagonal lines. Press and remove the papers to
make eight half-square-triangle units. The units

should measure 2" square, including seam
allowances. Make 168 A units.

Make 168 units,
2" × 2".

3 Repeat steps 1 and 2 using the tan floral and
remaining dark 5" squares. Make 56 B units
measuring 2" square, including seam allowances.

Make 56 units,
2" × 2".

MAKING THE BLOCKS

1 To make a side block, lay out four matching A units to form a pinwheel center, then add 10 assorted A units and two assorted B units to make four rows as shown. Sew the units together into rows. Join the rows to make a block measuring 6½" square, including seam allowances. Make six side blocks.

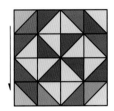

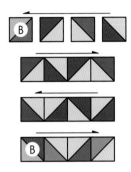

Side block.
Make 6 blocks,
6½" × 6½".

2 To make a corner block, lay out four matching A units to form a pinwheel center, then add nine assorted A units and three assorted B units to make four rows as shown. Sew the units together into rows. Join the rows to make a block measuring 6½" square, including seam allowances. Make four corner blocks.

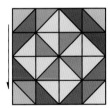

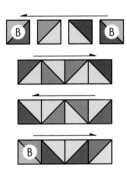

Corner block.
Make 4 blocks,
6½" × 6½".

3 To make a center top block, lay out a tan 2" × 3½" rectangle, two different B units, two different A units, and two matching A units in four rows. Sew the units together into rows. Join the rows to make a block measuring 3½" × 6½", including seam allowances. Repeat to make a center bottom block.

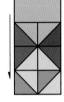

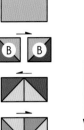

Center top/bottom block.
Make 2 blocks,
3½" × 6½".

4 To make a center block, arrange two sets of two matching A units (one set should match one block from step 3) and four assorted A units in four rows as shown. Sew the units together into rows. Join the rows to make a block measuring 3½" × 6½", including seam allowances. Make three blocks, referring to the quilt assembly diagram on page 31 as needed for fabric placement.

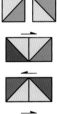

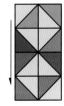

Center block.
Make 3 blocks,
3½" × 6½".

MAKING THE PIECED BORDER

1 Join two B units to make a border unit measuring 2" × 3½", including seam allowances. Make 14 border units.

Make 14 units,
2" × 3½".

2 Join two tan 2" squares, four tan 2" × 3½" rectangles, and five border units to make a side border measuring 2" × 30½", including seam allowances. Make two side borders.

Side border.
Make 2 borders,
2" × 30½".

3 Join two tan 2" × 3½" rectangles, one tan 2" × 6½" rectangle, and two border units to make the top border measuring 2" × 18½", including seam allowances. Repeat to make the bottom border.

Top/bottom border.
Make 2 borders,
2" × 18½".

ASSEMBLING THE QUILT TOP

1 Lay out the corner, side, center, center top, and center bottom blocks in five rows of three each as shown in the quilt assembly diagram below. Sew the blocks together into rows. Join the rows to make the quilt-top center, which should measure 15½" × 30½", including seam allowances.

2 Sew the 30½"-long pieced borders to opposite sides of the quilt top. Sew the 18½"-long pieced borders to the top and bottom of the quilt top. The quilt top should measure 18½" × 33½", including seam allowances.

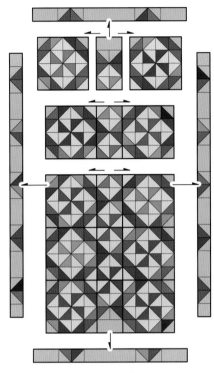

Quilt assembly

3 Sew the tan 33½"-long strips to opposite sides of the quilt top. Sew the tan 22½"-long strips to the top and bottom. The quilt top should measure 22½" × 37½".

FINISHING THE QUILT

For help with any of the finishing steps, go to ShopMartingale.com/HowtoQuilt for free downloadable information.

1 Layer the quilt top, batting, and backing; baste.

2 Quilt by hand or machine. The quilt shown is machine quilted with a swirling pinwheel design in the tan background, ditch quilting around the pinwheels and blocks, and a grid in the tan floral border areas.

3 Use the red 2¼"-wide strips to make the binding, and then attach the binding to the quilt.

Secret Ingredients

from Lynne Hagmeier

Her fabrics may lean toward the primitive look, but when it comes to her methods for making quilts, it's tough to be more modern than Lynne Hagmeier (KTQuilts.com). When she's not sewing on papers, it's raw-edge layers she loves!

Three ingredients I have to have at the ready when I'm sewing are a Quilters Select rotary cutter, three wound bobbins, and Twizzlers.

My favorite mix of colors almost always includes red.

When a quilt design needs a little something extra, I love to mix in raw-edge appliqué.

One of the best mixes I buy is a mix of dark chocolate and pretzel M&M's.

If I made a mix tape, the artist whose music would be on it for sure is Pink.

Two things others like to mix—but I don't—are lime green and anything.

In a bowl of snack mix, my favorites are the garlic rounds, **and my least favorites are** the crumbs at the bottom of the bag.

The most common mix-up I make when sewing is running out of bobbin thread.

Stand mixer or hand mixer? Neither. I use my food processor.

rosebud pinwheels

designed and pieced by BRENDA RIDDLE

A rosebud by any other name would be just as sweet! With apologies to Shakespeare for the adaptation, we can't apologize for how irresistibly sweet this throw is. We can almost smell the June roses on the trellis when we look at it!

Finished quilt: **69" × 78"**
Finished block: **9" × 9"**

MATERIALS

Yardage is based on 42"-wide fabric and use of Cake Mix Recipe papers. Traditional cutting-method options can be found on page 95 but will require additional yardage.

◼ Cupcake Mix 1 (two packs)

87 squares, 5" × 5", of assorted prints for blocks and triangle border

5¾ yards of ivory solid for blocks, setting squares, and borders

⅝ yard of pink print for binding

4¾ yards of fabric for backing

75" × 84" piece of batting

CUTTING

From the ivory solid, cut:

11 strips, 5" × 42"; crosscut into 87 squares, 5" × 5"

11 strips, 2" × 42"; crosscut into:

- 84 rectangles, 2" × 5"
- 4 squares, 2" × 2"

6 strips, 9½" × 42"; crosscut into 21 squares, 9½" × 9½"

7 strips, 3½" × 42"

8 strips, 3¼" × 42"

From the pink print, cut:

8 strips, 2¼" × 42"

MAKING THE UNITS

This quilt uses Cupcake Mix 1, which yields one half-square-triangle unit, 3" × 3" finished, and four half-square-triangle units, 1½" × 1½" finished, per recipe paper. (You'll need 87 papers.) Press the seam allowances as indicated by the arrows.

1 Place each ivory 5" square on top of a print square, right sides together. Pin a Cupcake Mix recipe paper to the top of each pair. Stitch on the dotted lines as indicated on the paper.

2 Cut apart the stitched squares on the solid lines, cutting the long diagonal line first. Press and remove the papers to make one A unit measuring 3½" square, including seam allowances, and four B units measuring 2" square, including seam allowances. Make 87 of unit A and 348 of unit B.

Unit A.
Make 87 units,
3½" × 3½".

Unit B.
Make 348 units,
2" × 2".

MAKING THE BLOCKS

1 Join two assorted B units to make a two-patch unit measuring 2" × 3½", including seam allowances. Make 84 units. Set aside the remaining B units for the triangle border.

Make 84 units,
2" × 3½".

2 Sew together a two-patch unit from step 1, an ivory rectangle, and an A unit to make a block quadrant measuring 5" square, including seam allowances. Make 84 units. You'll have three A units left over for another project.

Make 84 units,
5" × 5".

3 Lay out four quadrants in two rows of two, rotating them as shown. Sew the units together into rows. Join the rows to make a block measuring 9½" square, including seam allowances. Make 21 blocks.

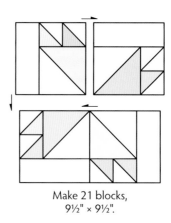

Make 21 blocks,
9½" × 9½".

MAKING THE TRIANGLE BORDER

1 Join 46 B units to make a side border measuring 2" × 69½", including seam allowances. Make two borders.

Make 2 side borders,
2" × 69½".

2 Join 40 B units and two ivory 2" squares to make the top border measuring 2" × 63½", including seam allowances. Repeat to make the bottom border. You'll have eight B units left over for another project.

Make 2 top/bottom borders,
2" × 63½".

Quilted by Nicole Christoffersen of Kwilt It

Addicted to 5" charm packs? You'll need just a few additional squares if you choose to begin this quilt with two charm packs of assorted prints.

ASSEMBLING THE QUILT TOP

1 Lay out the blocks and ivory 9½" squares in seven rows, alternating them as shown in the quilt assembly diagram. Sew the blocks and squares into rows. Join the rows to make the quilt center, which should measure 54½" × 63½", including seam allowances.

2 Join the ivory 3½"-wide strips end to end. From the pieced strip, cut two 63½"-long strips and two 60½"-long strips. Sew the longer strips to opposite sides of the quilt center. Sew the shorter strips to the top and bottom of the quilt center. The quilt top should measure 60½" × 69½", including seam allowances.

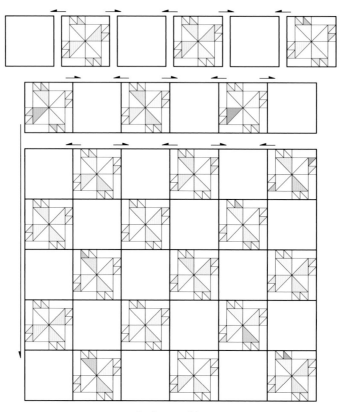

Quilt assembly

3 Sew the side triangle borders to opposite sides of the quilt top. Sew the top and bottom triangle borders to the quilt top, which should measure 63½" × 72½", including seam allowances.

4 Join the ivory 3¼"-wide strips end to end. From the pieced strip, cut two 72½"-long strips and two 69"-long strips. Sew the longer strips to opposite sides of the quilt top. Sew the shorter strips to the top and bottom of the quilt top. The quilt top should measure 69" × 78".

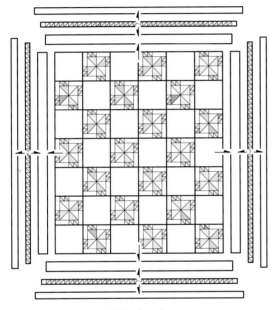

Adding borders

FINISHING THE QUILT

For help with any of the finishing steps, go to ShopMartingale.com/HowtoQuilt for free downloadable information.

1 Layer the quilt top, batting, and backing; baste.

2 Quilt by hand or machine. The quilt shown is machine quilted with an allover floral design.

3 Use the pink 2¼"-wide strips to make the binding, and then attach the binding to the quilt.

Secret Ingredients
from Brenda Riddle

From tiny Acorn Quilt & Gift Company come mighty designs! That's the saying, right? Well, we think so! Brenda Riddle (BrendaRiddleDesigns.com) is the might behind the soft and subtle beauties that are her quilts.

Three ingredients I have to have at the ready when I'm sewing are lots of prewound bobbins, the Hallmark Channel, and coffee!

My favorite mix of colors almost always includes soft white, light green, and warm light gray.

When a quilt design needs a little something extra, I love to mix in touches of embroidery or appliqué.

One of the best mixes I buy is Hidden Valley Ranch Seasoning Mix.

If I made a mix tape, the artist whose music would be on it for sure is Chris Tomlin.

When it comes to mixing it up in the kitchen, two unlikely things I like to mix together are peanut butter (crunchy, please) and dill pickles.

Two things others like to mix—but I don't—are chocolate and peanut butter.

In a bowl of snack mix, my favorites are the pretzels and garlic rounds, **and my least favorites are** the mini breadsticks.

The most common mix-up I make when sewing is not knowing what time it really is. I get lost in sewing and lose track!

Stand mixer or hand mixer? A stand mixer (a pink KitchenAid and I love her!).

square dance

designed by JANET CLARE

Just like learning dance steps where precision is important, you can maximize your precision in piecing by beginning with Cake Mix papers. Your triangle-squares will be properly pieced and spot on every time, resulting in complex-looking blocks and sashing that are a breeze to create.

Finished quilt: **54½" × 54½"**
Finished block: **12" × 12"**

MATERIALS

Yardage is based on 42"-wide fabric and use of Cake Mix Recipe papers. Traditional cutting-method options can be found on page 95 but will require additional yardage.

 Cake Mix 7 (one pack)

44 squares, 10" × 10", of assorted navy prints
   for blocks
3½ yards of cream solid for blocks
½ yard of navy print for binding
3½ yards of fabric for backing
61" × 61" piece of batting

CUTTING

From the cream solid, cut:
11 strips, 10" × 42"; crosscut into 44 squares,
   10" × 10"

From the navy print for binding, cut:
6 strips, 2¼" × 42"

MAKING THE UNITS

This quilt uses Cake Mix 7, which yields four half-square-triangle units, 3" × 3" finished, and 16 half-square-triangle units, 1½" × 1½" finished, per recipe paper. (You'll need 44 papers.) Press the seam allowances as indicated by the arrows.

1 Place each cream square on top of a navy square, right sides together. Pin a Cake Mix recipe paper to the top of each pair. Stitch on the dotted lines as indicated on the paper.

2 Cut apart the stitched squares on the solid lines. Press and remove the papers to make four A units measuring 3½" square, including seam allowances, and 16 B units measuring 2" square, including seam allowances. Make 176 of unit A and 704 of unit B.

Unit A.
Make 176 units,
3½" × 3½".

Unit B.
Make 704 units,
2" × 2".

MAKING THE BLOCKS

1 Lay out 16 B units in four rows of four. Sew the units together into rows. Join the rows to make a center unit measuring 6½" square, including seam allowances. Make nine units.

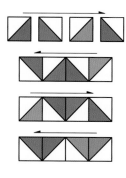

Make 9 units,
6½" × 6½".

2 Join two A units to make a side unit measuring 3½" × 6½", including seam allowances. Make 36 units.

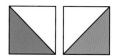

Make 36 units,
3½" × 6½".

3 Lay out four A units, four side units, and one center unit in three rows. Sew the units into rows. Join the rows to make a block measuring 12½" square, including seam allowances. Make nine blocks.

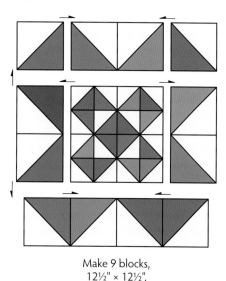

Make 9 blocks,
12½" × 12½".

MAKING THE DIAMOND SASHING

1 Sew together four B units to make a diamond unit measuring 3½" square, including seam allowances. Make 112 units. You'll have 112 B units leftover for another project.

Make 112 units,
3½" × 3½".

2 Join four diamond units to make a vertical sashing strip measuring 3½" × 12½", including seam allowances. Make 12 strips.

Make 12 strips,
3½" × 12½".

3 Join 16 diamond units to make a horizontal sashing strip measuring 3½" × 48½", including seam allowances. Make four strips.

Make 4 strips,
3½" × 48½".

MAKING THE TRIANGLE BORDERS

1 Join 16 A units, noting the orientation of the units, to make a side border measuring 3½" × 48½", including seam allowances. Make two side borders.

Make 1 left border,
3½" × 48½".

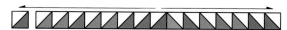

Make 1 right border,
3½" × 48½".

Pieced by Marion Bedford; quilted by Carolyn Clark

*Be mindful of the direction you're turning the triangle-squares when joining
the borders, noting the center points of each where the blue triangles meet.*

Secret Ingredients

from Janet Clare

It's hard to imagine Janet Clare (JanetClare.co.uk) without picturing her wearing her embellished apron, embroidered with any number of happy motifs and memories. When she's got it on, she's nearly always cooking up something exciting in her sewing room.

Three ingredients I have to have at the ready when I'm sewing are a cup of tea, my iron, and some music.

My favorite mix of colors almost always includes blue.

When a quilt design needs a little something extra, I love to mix in an embroidered word or saying.

One of the best mixes I buy is nothing. I never buy mixes.

If I made a mix tape, the artist whose music would be on it for sure is Adele.

When it comes to mixing it up in the kitchen, two unlikely things I like to mix together are courgette (zucchini) and lime. It makes a mean cake!

Two things others like to mix—but I don't—are peanut butter and jelly. Why do people do that?

In a bowl of snack mix, I'll leave behind all the dried-out bread.

The most common mix-up I make when sewing is the order of my rows after too much speedy chain piecing.

Stand mixer or hand mixer? Stand mixer. I bought it with the royalties from my first book!

2 Join 18 A units, noting the orientation of the units, to make the top border measuring 3½" × 54½", including seam allowances. Repeat to make the bottom border.

Make 2 top/bottom borders,
3½" × 54½".

ASSEMBLING THE QUILT TOP

1 Join three blocks and four vertical sashing strips to make a row measuring 12½" × 48½", including seam allowances. Make three rows.

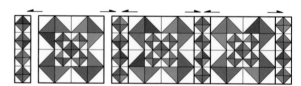

Make 3 rows,
12½" × 48½".

2 Lay out the block rows and horizontal sashing strips as shown in the quilt assembly diagram below. Sew the rows together to make the quilt-top center, which should measure 48½" square, including seam allowances.

3 Sew the 48½"-long triangle borders to opposite sides of the quilt top. Sew the 54½"-long triangle borders to the top and bottom of the quilt top. The quilt should measure 54½" square.

FINISHING THE QUILT

For help with any of the finishing steps, go to ShopMartingale.com/HowtoQuilt for free downloadable information.

1 Layer the quilt top, batting, and backing; baste.

2 Quilt by hand or machine. The quilt shown is machine quilted with a swirling pinwheel design.

3 Use the navy 2¼"-wide strips to make the binding, and then attach the binding to the quilt.

Quilt assembly

quilter's confetti

designed and pieced by KRISTYNE CZEPURYK

Talk about sparkle! This quilt is like a party for pretty prints. Mix and match 10" Layer Cake squares from different fabric lines to expand the variety of colorful prints in this cozy throw. Want an instant scrappy masterpiece? Start with four Layer Cakes total. Aside from the backing and binding, those are the only fabrics used in this stunning scrap quilt. Edge to edge, it's downright scraptastic!

Finished quilt: **64½" × 72½"**
Finished block: **8" × 8"**

MATERIALS

Yardage is based on 42"-wide fabric and use of Cake Mix Recipe papers. Traditional cutting-method options can be found on page 95 but will require additional yardage.

⬛ Cake Mix 8 (two packs)

72 squares, 10" × 10", of assorted light prints for
    blocks
72 squares, 10" × 10", of assorted medium and dark
    prints for blocks (referred to collectively as "dark")
⅝ yard of white solid for binding
4 yards of fabric for backing
71" × 79" piece of batting

CUTTING

From the white solid, cut:
8 strips, 2¼" × 42"

MAKING THE UNITS

This quilt uses Cake Mix 8, which yields four half-square-triangle units, 3" × 3" finished, and 30 half-square-triangle units, 1" × 1" finished, per recipe paper. (You'll need 72 papers.) Press the seam allowances as indicated by the arrows.

1 Place each light square on top of a dark square, right sides together. Pin a Cake Mix recipe paper to the top of each pair. Stitch on the dotted lines as indicated on the paper.

2 Cut apart the stitched squares on the solid lines, starting with the horizontal and vertical lines. Press and remove the papers to make 30 A units measuring 1½" square, including seam

allowances, and four B units measuring 3½"
square, including seam allowances. Make 2160
of unit A and 288 of unit B.

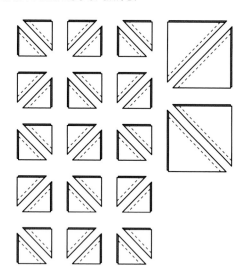

Unit A.
Make 2160 units,
1½" × 1½".

Unit B.
Make 288 units,
3½" × 3½".

MAKING THE BLOCKS

1 Join two A units to make a C unit measuring
1½" × 2½", including seam allowances. Make 504
of unit C, making sure the dark triangles are on
the outer corners.

Unit C.
Make 504 units,
1½" × 2½".

2 Join two A units to make a D unit measuring
1½" × 2½", including seam allowances. Make 504
of unit D, making sure the light triangles are on
the outer corners. You'll have 144 A units left over.

Unit D.
Make 504 units,
1½" × 2½".

3 Join three different C units to make a C side
unit measuring 2½" × 3½", including seam
allowances. Make 72 units, with the dark triangles
on the outer edges.

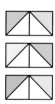

Side unit.
Make 72 units,
2½" × 3½".

4 Join eight different C units to make a C center row
measuring 2½" × 8½", including seam allowances.
Make 36 rows.

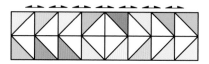

Center row.
Make 36 rows,
2½" × 8½".

5 Lay out four different B units, two C side units,
and one C center row in three rows as shown. Sew
the pieces together into rows. Join the rows to
make a block measuring 8½" square, including
seam allowances. Make 36 of block C, with the
dark triangles on the outer edges.

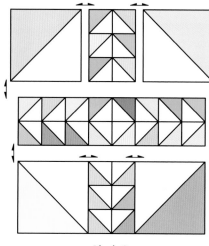

Block C.
Make 36 blocks,
8½" × 8½".

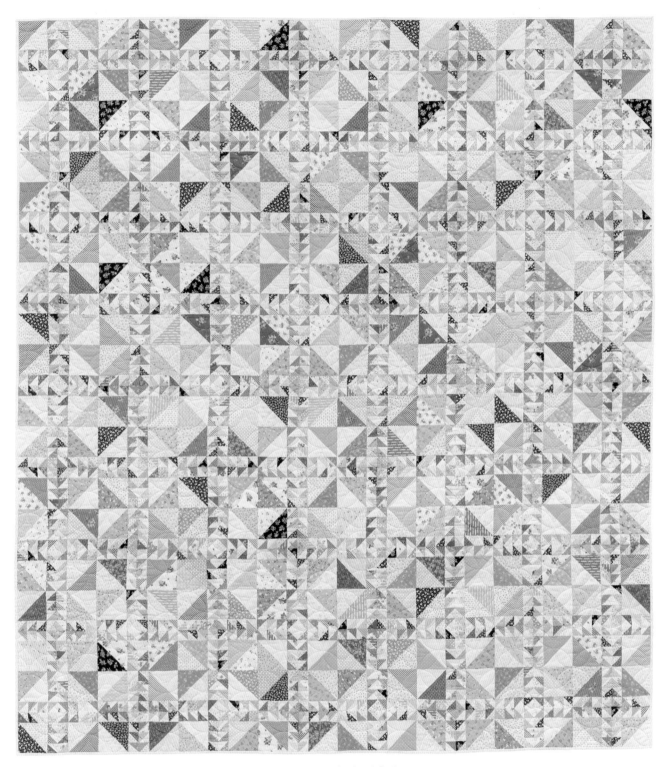

Quilted by Judy Gugielmin

Before joining the blocks into rows, lay them out to see how dominant colors are distributed across the quilt. Rotate and adjust placement until you're pleased.

Secret Ingredients

from Kristyne Czepuryk

It's not a secret that pink is pretty much Kristyne Czepuryk's (PrettyByHand.com) favorite color. It keeps popping up in her quilts. But here's another secret—we're in love with the look!

Three ingredients I have to have at the ready when I'm sewing are good lighting, loaded bobbins, and an awesome playlist.

My favorite mix of colors almost always includes white and pink.

When a quilt design needs a little something extra, I love to mix in embroidery.

One of the best mixes I buy is Ghirardelli Double Chocolate brownie mix. Oh. My. Word.

If I made a mix tape, the artist whose music would be on it for sure is Def Leppard (embarrassing, but true). And Depeche Mode. And Foreigner.

When it comes to mixing it up in the kitchen, two unlikely things I like to mix together are apple slices and powdered peanut butter. Trust me, it's delicious.

Two things others like to mix—but I don't—is anything with mushrooms.

In a bowl of snack mix, my favorites are the cashews and chocolate chips, **and my least favorites are** the raisins and Brazil nuts.

The most common mix-up I make when sewing is *everything!* Oh gosh, the older I get, the more varied and frequent my sewing mix-ups are. You name it, I've done it!

Stand mixer or hand mixer? A stand mixer. I love my KitchenAid that was a wedding gift 23 years ago. It has never let me down.

6. Join three different D units to make a D side unit measuring 2½" × 3½", including seam allowances. Make 72 units, with the light triangles on the outer edges.

Side unit.
Make 72 units,
2½" × 3½".

7. Join eight different D units to make a D center row measuring 2½" × 8½", including seam allowances. Make 36 rows.

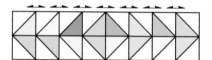

Center row.
Make 36 rows,
2½" × 8½".

8. Lay out four different B units, two D side units, and one D center row in three rows as shown. Sew the pieces together into rows. Join the rows to make a block measuring 8½" square, including seam allowances. Make 36 of block D, with the light triangles on the outer edges.

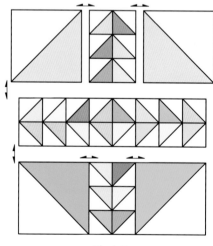

Block D.
Make 36 blocks,
8½" × 8½".

ASSEMBLING THE QUILT TOP

Lay out the C and D blocks in nine rows of eight blocks each, alternating the blocks in each row and from row to row as shown in the quilt assembly diagram. Sew the blocks together into rows. Join the rows to complete the quilt top. The quilt top should measure 64½" × 72½".

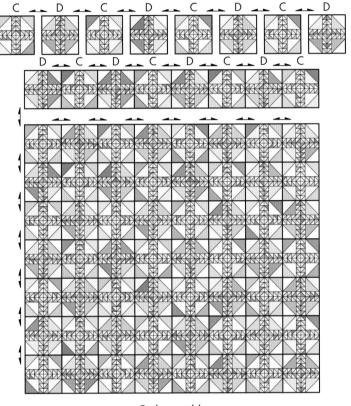

Quilt assembly

FINISHING THE QUILT

For help with any of the finishing steps, go to ShopMartingale.com/HowtoQuilt for free downloadable information.

1. Layer the quilt top, batting, and backing; baste.

2. Quilt by hand or machine. The quilt shown is machine quilted with an allover orange peel design.

3. Use the white 2¼"-wide strips to make the binding, and then attach the binding to the quilt.

step it up

designed, pieced, and quilted by BETSY CHUTCHIAN

Are you ready to up your patchwork game? Here's a brain teaser. When do two and eighteen equal the same result? When you're making 3" blocks for this two-block beauty. One block has two pieces. The other has 18. How can you ever make a little block with that many pieces? Simple. Sew on the lines of your Cake Mix and you'll have all the little half-square triangles you need completed in no-time!

Finished quilt: **36½" × 42½"**
Finished block: **3" × 3"**

MATERIALS

Yardage is based on 42"-wide fabric and use of Cake Mix Recipe papers. Traditional cutting-method options can be found on page 95 but will require additional yardage.

▪ Cake Mix 8 (one pack)

26 squares, 10" × 10", of assorted cream prints
    for blocks
13 squares, 10" × 10", of assorted navy prints
    for blocks
7 squares, 10" × 10", of assorted brown prints
    for blocks
6 squares, 10" × 10", of assorted red prints
    for blocks
¼ yard of red solid for binding
2½ yards of fabric for backing
43" × 49" piece of batting

CUTTING

From the red solid, cut:
5 strips, 1⅛" × 42"

MAKING THE UNITS

This quilt uses Cake Mix 8, which yields four half-square-triangle units, 3" × 3" finished, and 30 half-square-triangle units, 1" × 1" finished, per recipe paper. (You'll need 26 papers.) Press the seam allowances as indicated by the arrows.

1 Place a cream square on top of each navy square, right sides together. Pin a Cake Mix paper to the top of each pair. Stitch on the dotted lines as indicated on the paper.

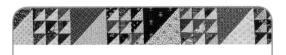

light on top

Why sew with the light fabric on top? That way, when you press the units open before removing the paper, the seams will automatically be pressed toward the dark fabric.

2 Cut apart the stitched squares on the solid lines, starting with the horizontal and vertical lines. Press and remove the papers to make 30 A units measuring 1½" square, including seam allowances,

and four B units measuring 3½" square, including seam allowances. Repeat to make 390 of unit A and 52 of unit B.

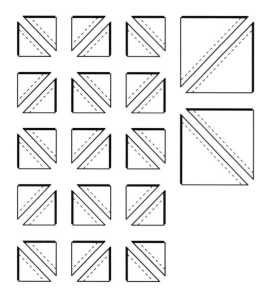

Unit A.
Make 390 units,
1½" × 1½".

Unit B.
Make 52 units,
3½" × 3½".

3 Repeat steps 1 and 2 using the cream and red squares to make 180 of unit A and 24 of unit B. Use the remaining cream squares and the brown squares to make 210 of unit A and 28 of unit B.

Unit A.
Make 180 units,
1½" × 1½".

Unit B.
Make 24 units,
3½" × 3½".

Unit A.
Make 210 units,
1½" × 1½".

Unit B.
Make 28 units,
3½" × 3½".

MAKING THE BLOCKS

Lay out nine blue A units in three rows of three. Sew the units together into rows. Join the rows to make a block measuring 3½" square, including seam allowances. Make 42 blue blocks. Repeat to make 20 red blocks and 22 brown blocks. You'll have 12 blue units and 12 brown units left over for another project.

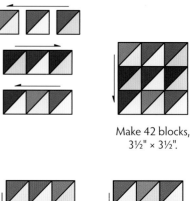

Make 42 blocks,
3½" × 3½".

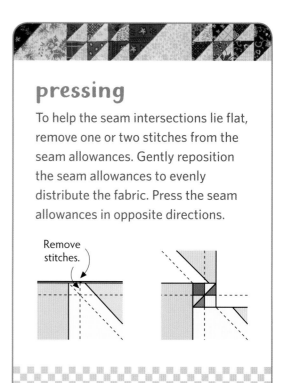

Make 20 blocks,
3½" × 3½".

Make 22 blocks,
3½" × 3½".

pressing

To help the seam intersections lie flat, remove one or two stitches from the seam allowances. Gently reposition the seam allowances to evenly distribute the fabric. Press the seam allowances in opposite directions.

Remove stitches.

Diagonal designs often fool the eye, making you think they're pieced in diagonal rows. In fact, it's an illusion. The blocks in this stunner are simply set side-by-side.

Secret Ingredients

from Betsy Chutchian

Even though she really loves reproduction prints and classic blocks, Betsy Chutchian (BetsysBestQuiltsandMore.blogspot.com) also embraces today's tools and techniques when making her quilts, which are reminiscent of those from the nineteenth century.

Three ingredients I have to have at the ready when I'm sewing are a really hot iron, a seam ripper, and a Netflix series playing near the sewing machine.

My favorite mix of colors almost always includes some indigo.

When a quilt design needs a little something extra, I mix in a little pop of color—double pink, poison green, or robin's egg blue.

One of the best mixes I buy is Krusteaz Traditional Scone Mix.

If I made a mix tape, the artist whose music would be on it for sure is whichever artist my kids think I'd like, since they'd be making the tape.

When it comes to mixing it up in the kitchen, unlikely things I like to mix together are popcorn, dill pickles, and cheddar cheese (aka Sunday Supper at my house).

Two things others like to mix—but I don't—are pink and purple.

In a bowl of snack mix, my favorites are the Wheat Chex and garlic bagel rounds, **and my least favorites are** the peanuts!

The most common mix-up I make when sewing is forgetting to unplug the iron.

Stand mixer or hand mixer? Stand mixer (a KitchenAid).

ASSEMBLING THE QUILT TOP

1 Lay out the blocks and B units in 14 rows of 12, alternating them in each row and from row to row as shown in the quilt assembly diagram below to create diagonal bands of color. Sew the blocks and units together into rows. You'll have 10 blue, three red, and seven brown B units left over for another project.

2 Join the rows to complete the quilt top. The quilt top should measure 36½" × 42½".

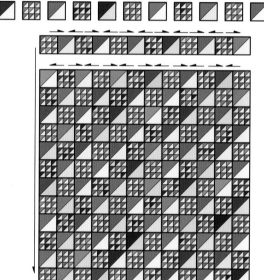

Quilt assembly

FINISHING THE QUILT

For help with any of the finishing steps, go to ShopMartingale.com/HowtoQuilt for free downloadable information.

1 Layer the quilt top, batting, and backing; baste.

2 Quilt by hand or machine. The quilt shown features machine quilting in the ditch.

3 Use the red 1⅛"-wide strips to make single-fold binding, and then attach the binding to the quilt.

frosty days

designed by ANNE SUTTON

Location, location, location! Just as in real estate, location is the key to success with this wintry table topper. The position of your background fabric in the star blocks and pinwheel blocks allows a secondary pattern to emerge, making it difficult to determine where one block ends and the next begins. Brilliant!

Finished quilt: **42½" × 42½"**
Finished block: **6" × 6"**

MATERIALS

Yardage is based on 42"-wide fabric and use of Cake Mix Recipe papers. Traditional cutting-method options can be found on page 95 but will require additional yardage.

Cupcake Mix 2 *and* **Cupcake Mix 4** (one pack of each)

34 squares, 5" × 5", of assorted prints for Star blocks
8 squares, 5" × 5", of assorted prints for triangle border
16 pairs of matching squares, 5" × 5" (32 total), of assorted prints for Pinwheel blocks
2⅛ yards of ivory solid for blocks, first border, and third border
½ yard of red solid for binding
2¾ yards of fabric for backing
49" × 49" piece of batting

CUTTING

From the ivory solid, cut:
10 strips, 5" × 42"; crosscut into 73 squares, 5" × 5"
2 strips, 2" × 42"; crosscut into:
  * 2 strips, 2" × 18½"
  * 2 strips, 2" × 21½"
4 strips, 3½" × 42"; crosscut into:
  * 2 strips, 3½" × 24½"
  * 2 strips, 3½" × 30½"

From the red solid, cut:
5 strips, 2¼" × 42"

MAKING THE UNITS

This quilt uses Cupcake Mix 2, which yields eight half-square-triangle units, 1½" × 1½" finished, per recipe paper. It also uses Cupcake Mix 4, which yields four half-square-triangle units, 1½" × 1½" finished, and four squares, 1½" × 1½" finished, per recipe paper. (You'll need 39 Cupcake Mix 2 papers and 34 Cupcake Mix 4 papers.) Press the seam allowances as indicated by the arrows.

1 Place an ivory square on top of each of the 34 assorted print 5" squares for Star blocks, right sides together. Pin a Cupcake Mix 4 recipe paper to the top of each pair. Stitch on the dotted lines as indicated on the paper.

2 Cut apart the stitched squares on the solid lines. Press and remove the papers to make four A units measuring 2" square, including seam allowances, and four 2" squares. Make 136 of unit A. You'll have 68 print squares and 68 ivory squares for making the Star blocks.

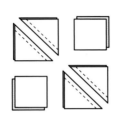

Unit A.
Make 136 units,
2" × 2".

Make 68 of each unit,
2" × 2".

3 Using the 16 pairs of matching 5" squares, place an ivory square on top of each print square, right sides together. Pin a Cupcake Mix 2 recipe paper to the top of each pair. Stitch on the dotted lines as indicated on the recipe paper.

4 Cut the stitched squares apart on the solid lines, starting with the horizontal and vertical lines. Trim on the outside 4¾" line and then cut on the solid diagonal lines. Press and remove the papers to make eight B units measuring 2" square, including seam allowances. Make 256 of unit B, keeping matching units together.

Unit B.
Make 256 units,
2" × 2".

5 Repeat steps 3 and 4 using seven of the assorted print 5" squares for the triangle border and the remaining ivory squares to make 56 C units measuring 2" square, including seam allowances.

Unit C.
Make 56 units,
2" × 2".

MAKING THE BLOCKS

1 For one Star block, you'll need two sets of four matching A units, two pairs of print 2" squares that match the units, and four ivory squares from step 2 of "Making the Units." Lay out the pieces in four rows of four. Sew the pieces together into rows. Join the rows to make a Star block measuring 6½" square, including seam allowances. Make 17 blocks.

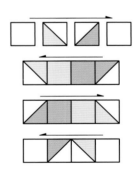

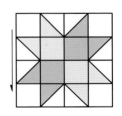

Star block.
Make 17 blocks,
6½" × 6½".

Pieced by Nancy Ritter; quilted by Maggi Honeyman

Tired of winter decor that looks out of step by mid-January? Go upscale and timeless with a sophisticated mix of winter whites, cranberry reds, and icy blues.

2 For one Pinwheel block, lay out 12 matching B units and four matching B units from a different print in four rows of four. Sew the units together into rows. Join the rows to make a Pinwheel block measuring 6½" square, including seam allowances. Make 16 blocks.

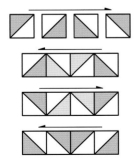
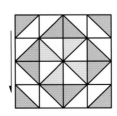

Pinwheel block.
Make 16 blocks,
6½" × 6½".

MAKING THE TRIANGLE BORDER

1 Join 14 C units to make a side border measuring 2" × 21½", including seam allowances. Make two.

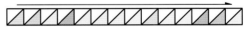

Side border.
Make 2 borders, 2" × 21½".

2 Cut the remaining print 5" square into four 2" squares. Join 14 C units and two 2" squares to make the top border measuring 2" × 24½", including seam allowances. Repeat to make the bottom border.

Top/bottom border.
Make 2 borders, 2" × 24½".

Secret Ingredients

from Anne Sutton

Put your right foot forward, put your left foot out, and do the bunny hop right over to Anne Sutton and Bunny Hill Designs (BunnyHillDesigns.com). She's got a great eye for color and a heart of gold.

Three ingredients I have to have at the ready when I'm sewing are scissors, a pincushion, and television recordings of Grey's Anatomy.

My favorite mix of colors almost always includes shades of pink.

When a quilt design needs a little something extra, I mix in fabric that's brighter than the other fabrics already in the quilt.

One of the best mixes I buy is King Arthur Cranberry Orange Scone Mix.

If I made a mix tape, the artist whose music would be on it for sure is Josh Groban.

When it comes to mixing it up in the kitchen, two unlikely things I like to mix together are cheese and jam.

Two things others like to mix—but I don't—are pizza and anchovies.

In a bowl of snack mix, my favorites are the nuts and bagel bits, **and my least favorite is** the Chex cereal.

The most common mix-up I make when sewing is forgetting to turn off the iron. Thank goodness for auto shutoff!

Stand mixer or hand mixer? KitchenAid stand mixer all the way.

ASSEMBLING THE QUILT TOP

Refer to the quilt assembly diagram on page 61 as needed for placement guidance.

1. Lay out five Star blocks and four Pinwheel blocks in three rows of three. Sew the blocks together into rows. Join the rows to make the quilt center, which should measure 18½" square, including seam allowances.

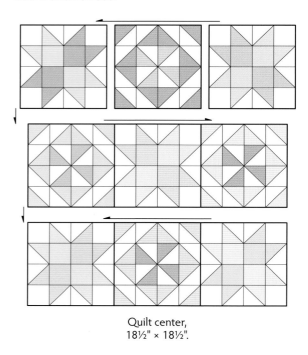

Quilt center,
18½" × 18½".

2. Sew the ivory 2" × 18½" strips to opposite sides of the quilt center. Sew the ivory 2" × 21½" strips to the top and bottom of the quilt center. The quilt top should measure 21½" square, including seam allowances.

3. Sew the 21½"-long triangle borders to opposite sides of the quilt top. Sew the 24½"-long triangle borders to the top and bottom of the quilt top, which should measure 24½" square, including seam allowances.

4. Sew the ivory 3½" × 24½" strips to opposite sides of the quilt top. Sew the ivory 3½" × 30½" strips to the top and bottom of the quilt top, which should measure 30½" square, including seam allowances.

5 Join three Pinwheel blocks and two Star blocks to make a side outer border measuring 6½" × 30½", including seam allowances. Make two.

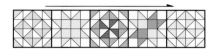

Side outer border.
Make 2 borders, 6½" × 30½".

6 Join four Star blocks and three Pinwheel blocks to make the top outer border, which should measure 6½" × 42½", including seam allowances. Repeat to make the bottom outer border.

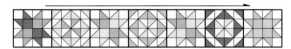

Top/bottom outer border.
Make 2 borders, 6½" × 42½".

7 Sew the shorter outer borders to opposite sides of the quilt top and the longer outer borders to the top and bottom of the quilt top. The quilt top should measure 42½" square.

FINISHING THE QUILT

For help with any of the finishing steps, go to ShopMartingale.com/HowtoQuilt for free downloadable information.

1 Layer the quilt top, batting, and backing; baste.

2 Hand or machine quilt. The quilt shown is machine quilted with orange peels and straight lines in the Star blocks, along with feathers and straight lines in the Pinwheel blocks. A swirl design is quilted in the narrow ivory border and feathers fill the wider ivory border.

3 Use the red 2¼"-wide strips to make the binding, and then attach the binding to the quilt.

Quilt assembly

piping hot

designed, pieced, and quilted by SANDY KLOP

Many quilters confess to being a bit intimidated by sewing triangles. Well, if you can sew on a line, you can (and should!) make this quilt. And once you do, you'll soon forget you ever had a fear of triangles. The secret to re-creating the design begins with pairs of matching charm squares. Pair up those prints, partner them with solid red, and you're ready to sit down and sew!

Finished quilt: **60" × 60"**
Finished block: **6" × 6"**

MATERIALS

Yardage is based on 42"-wide fabric and use of Cake Mix Recipe papers. Traditional cutting-method options can be found on page 95 but will require additional yardage.

 Cupcake Mix 2 (three packs)

57 pairs of matching squares, 5" × 5" (114 total), of assorted prints for blocks
14 squares, 5" × 5", of assorted prints for blocks
3⅜ yards of red solid for blocks, setting triangles, and binding
1¼ yards of white print for blocks
3¾ yards of fabric for backing
66" × 66" piece of batting

CUTTING

From the red solid, cut:
15 strips, 5" × 42"; crosscut into 114 squares, 5" × 5"
2 strips, 9¾" × 42; crosscut into:
  • 6 squares, 9¾" × 9¾"; cut the squares into quarters diagonally to yield 24 side triangles
  • 2 squares, 5⅛" × 5⅛"; cut the squares in half diagonally to yield 4 corner triangles
7 strips, 2¼" × 42"

From the white print, cut:
2 strips, 5" × 42"; crosscut into 14 squares, 5" × 5"
3 strips, 6½" × 42"; crosscut into 56 rectangles, 2" × 6½"
3 strips, 3½" × 42"; crosscut into 56 rectangles, 2" × 3½"

MAKING THE UNITS

This quilt uses Cupcake Mix 2, which yields eight half-square-triangle units, 1½" × 1½" finished, per recipe paper. (You'll need 128 papers.) Press the seam allowances as indicated by the arrows.

1 Layer each of the matching 5" squares with a red square, right sides together and with the lighter square on top. Pin a Cupcake Mix recipe paper to the top of each pair. Stitch on the dotted lines as indicated on the paper.

Secret Ingredients

from Sandy Klop

Oh, Sandy, you're so fine! You're so fine, you blow our minds! Sandy Klop (AmericanJane.com) brings her A-game to every quilt she makes. Here's what's cookin' with her.

An ingredient I have to have at the ready when I'm sewing is my scissors!

My favorite mix of colors almost always includes red, yellow, blue, and green . . . and sometimes orange!

When a quilt design needs a little something extra, I mix in a special border treatment.

One of the best mixes I buy is Chex Mix.

If I made a mix tape, the artists whose music would be on it for sure are Queen and Greg Champion.

When it comes to mixing it up in the kitchen, two unlikely things I like to mix together are pepper jelly on a grilled cheese sandwich.

In a bowl of snack mix, my favorites are the pretzels **and my least favorites are** the hazelnuts.

The most common mix-up I make when I'm sewing is stitching without bobbin thread!

Stand mixer or hand mixer? Hand mixer. We received a stand mixer for a wedding gift, but we returned it for a hand mixer . . . and then had extra money!

2 Cut apart the stitched squares on the solid lines, starting with the horizontal and vertical lines. Trim on the outside 4¾" line and then cut on the solid diagonal lines. Press and remove the papers to make eight A units measuring 2" square, including seam allowances. Make 912 of unit A.

Unit A.
Make 912 units,
2" × 2".

3 Repeat steps 1 and 2 using the 14 assorted print 5" squares and the white squares to make 112 B units measuring 2" square, including seam allowances.

Unit B.
Make 112 units,
2" × 2".

MAKING THE BLOCKS

1 Lay out 16 matching A units in four rows of four units each, noting the orientation of the units. Sew the units together into rows. Join the rows to make a block measuring 6½" square, including seam allowances. Make 57 of block A.

 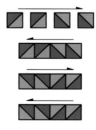

Block A.
Make 57 blocks,
6½" × 6½".

2 Arrange four different B units in two rows of two, noting their orientation. Join the units into rows. Join the rows to make a pinwheel unit measuring

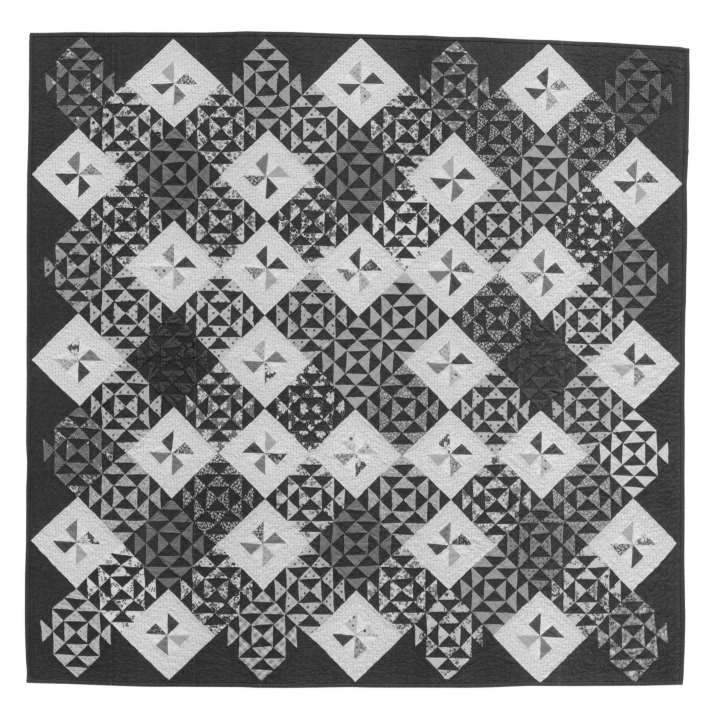

Who are you sayin' is solid? Nitsy prints (tiny motifs) read like solids from a distance. But once you're up close, you see their clever little designs.

3½" square, including seam allowances. Make 26 units and two reversed units.

Make 26 units, Make 2 reversed units,
3½" × 3½". 3½" × 3½".

3 Lay out two white 2" × 3½" rectangles, two white 2" × 6½" rectangles, and a pinwheel unit in three rows. Sew the pieces together into rows. Join the rows to make a block measuring 6½" square, including seam allowances. Make 26 of block B and two of block B reversed.

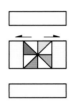

Block B. Block B reversed.
Make 26 blocks, Make 2 blocks,
6½" × 6½". 6½" × 6½".

ASSEMBLING THE QUILT TOP

Arrange the blocks, red side triangles, and red corner triangles in diagonal rows as shown in the quilt assembly diagram below. Sandy placed her reversed blocks in the fifth row and bottom row, but you can place yours as desired. Sew the pieces together into rows. Join the rows, adding the corner triangles last. The quilt top should measure 60" square.

FINISHING THE QUILT

For help with any of the finishing steps, go to ShopMartingale.com/HowtoQuilt for free downloadable information.

1 Layer the quilt top, batting, and backing; baste.

2 Quilt by hand or machine. The quilt shown is machine quilted with an allover meander design.

3 Use the red 2¼"-wide strips to make the binding, and then attach the binding to the quilt.

Quilt assembly

stormy day

Designed by LISA BONGEAN

Ocean Waves is a traditional quilt pattern packed with triangles. Do you find it somewhat daunting? Turn it into smooth sailing by stitching on Cake Mix 3 papers. And if quilting is your thing (or you have a fabulous quilter you rely on), you'll have plenty of wide-open spaces for showing off distinctive quilting designs.

Finished quilt: **90½" × 90½"**
Finished block: **18½" × 18½"**

MATERIALS

Yardage is based on 42"-wide fabric and use of Cake Mix Recipe papers. Traditional cutting-method options can be found on page 95 but will require additional yardage.

■ **Cake Mix 3** (two packs)

101 squares, 10" × 10", of assorted light, medium, and dark prints for blocks
4⅞ yards of gray solid for blocks and border
10 strips, 2¼" × 42", of assorted prints for scrappy binding*
8¼ yards of fabric for backing
99" × 99" piece of batting

*If you prefer to use one fabric for the binding, you'll need ¾ yard.

CUTTING

From *9* of the assorted print 10" squares, cut a *total* of:

80 squares, 2⅞" × 2⅞"; cut the squares in half diagonally to yield 160 triangles

From the *crosswise* grain of the gray solid, cut:

6 strips, 10⅞" × 42"; crosscut into 16 squares, 10⅞" × 10⅞". Cut the squares in half diagonally to yield 32 triangles.

From the *lengthwise* grain of the gray solid, cut:

2 strips, 9½" × 90½"
2 strips, 9½" × 72½"

MAKING THE UNITS

This quilt uses Cake Mix 3, which yields 18 half-square-triangle units, 2" × 2" finished, per recipe paper. (You'll need 46 papers.) Press the seam allowances as indicated by the arrows.

1 Organize the assorted print squares into pairs of nonmatching prints. Layer each pair, right sides together, with the lighter square on top. Pin a Cake Mix recipe paper to the top of each pair. Stitch on the dotted lines as indicated on the paper.

2 Cut apart the stitched squares on the solid lines, starting with the horizontal and vertical lines. Press and remove the papers to make 18 half-square-triangle units measuring 2½" square, including seam allowances. Make 828 units.

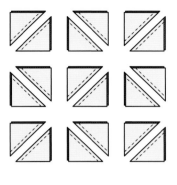

Make 828 units,
2½" × 2½".

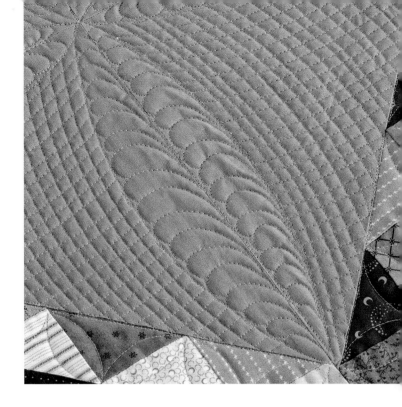

MAKING THE BLOCKS

1 Lay out 51 half-square-triangle units and 10 print triangles in nine rows. Sew the units and triangles together into rows. Join the rows to make a pieced unit. Make 16 units. You'll have 12 half-square-triangle units left over for another project.

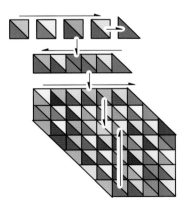

Make 16 units.

2 Sew gray triangles to opposite corners of a pieced unit to make a block measuring 18½" square, including seam allowances. Make 16 blocks.

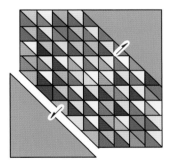

Make 16 blocks,
18½" × 18½".

Pieced by Lisa Bongean and Amy Hoefler;
quilted by Maggi Honeyman

*Don't stop the scrappiness with your blocks. Take it all the way to the edge and
add a scrappy binding to your project to finish it off with a hint of whimsy.*

ASSEMBLING THE QUILT TOP

1 Lay out the blocks in four rows of four blocks each, rotating them as shown in the quilt assembly diagram. Sew the blocks together into rows. Join the rows to complete the quilt-top center. The quilt top should measure 72½" square, including seam allowances.

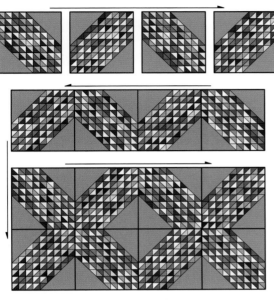

Quilt assembly

2 Sew the gray 72½"-long strips to opposite sides of the quilt top. Sew the gray 90½"-long strips to the top and bottom of the quilt top. The quilt top should measure 90½" square.

FINISHING THE QUILT

For help with any of the finishing steps, go to ShopMartingale.com/HowtoQuilt for free downloadable information.

1 Layer the quilt top, batting, and backing; baste.

2 Quilt by hand or machine. The quilt shown is machine quilted with curved crosshatching, feathers, and swirls.

3 Use the assorted print 2¼"-wide strips to make the binding, and then attach the binding to the quilt.

Secret Ingredients

from Lisa Bongean

Crisscross applesauce! We're gaga over Lisa Bongean's most "X"cellent quilt. But then again, we love every little thing she does—because she loves to sew little. Check out more of her genius at PrimitiveGatherings.us.

Three ingredients I have to have at the ready when I'm sewing are freshly wound bobbins, a new needle, and an audiobook. Plus, I have to start with a clean sewing studio!

My favorite mix of colors almost always includes gray with any two other colors. I'm currently obsessed with gray!

When a quilt design needs a little something extra, I love to mix in a little appliqué. Sometimes a little goes a long way.

One of the best mixes I don't buy, but rather make, is white chocolate raspberry scones *mixed* with my KitchenAid mixer. (How's that for bringing it all together?)

If I made a mix tape, the artist whose music would be on it for sure is Journey.

When it comes to mixing it up in the kitchen, two unlikely things I like to mix together are chili and beer.

Two things others like to mix—but I don't—are husbands and vacations!

In a bowl of snack mix, my favorites are the Chex cereal, pretzels, and garlic rounds, **and my least favorites are** the Bugles and breadsticks.

The most common mix-up I make when sewing is turning my blocks in the wrong direction when I'm sewing rows together.

Stand mixer or hand mixer? Definitely a stand mixer. I have a black one and a silver one!

candied cotton

designed and pieced by COREY YODER

Sweet as can be, this lap-size quilt has us making all the heart eyes. At a glance, squares and triangles seem to zig and zag across the quilt top, but don't be fooled. Upon closer inspection you'll see the design is nothing more than simple four-patches set with triangle squares in the block corners. Beginning with a Cake Mix, a Layer Cake of prints, and a Layer Cake of cream solid, it's 42 straight-set blocks of fun!

Finished Quilt: **54½" × 63½"**
Finished Block: **9" × 9"**

MATERIALS

Yardage is based on 42"-wide fabric and use of Cake Mix Recipe papers. Traditional cutting-method options can be found on page 95 but will require additional yardage.

 **Cake Mix 10** (one pack)

42 squares, 10" × 10", of assorted prints for blocks
42 squares, 10" × 10", of cream solid for blocks
½ yard of pink stripe for binding
3½ yards of fabric for backing
61" × 70" piece of batting

CUTTING

From the pink stripe, cut:
250" of 2¼"-wide bias strips

MAKING THE UNITS

This quilt uses Cake Mix 10, which yields four half-square-triangle units, 3" × 3" finished, and five four-patch units, 3" × 3" finished, per recipe paper. (You'll need 42 papers.) Press the seam allowances as indicated by the arrows.

1 Place a cream square on top of each assorted print square, right sides together. Pin a Cake Mix recipe paper to the top of each pair. Stitch on the dotted lines as indicated on the paper.

2 Cut apart the stitched squares on the solid lines. Press and remove the papers to make four half-square-triangle units measuring 3½" square, including seam allowances, and 10 two-patch units measuring 2" × 3½", including seam allowances. Make 168 half-square-triangle units and 420 two-patch units.

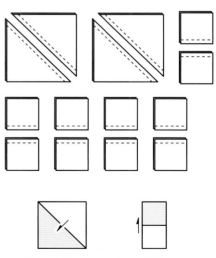

Make 168 units, 3½" × 3½".　　Make 420 units, 2" × 3½".

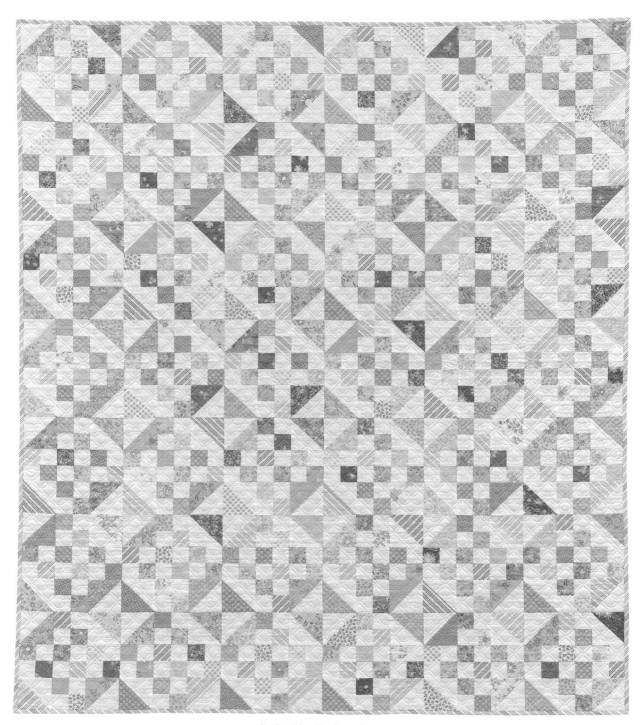

Quilted by Kaylene Parry

The beauty of beginning a quilt with Layer Cake precuts of 10" squares is that you have a guaranteed-to-go-together assortment of prints.

MAKING THE BLOCKS

1. Randomly sew a pair of two-patch units together to make a four-patch unit. Make a total of 210 units measuring 3½" square, including seam allowances.

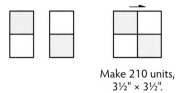

Make 210 units,
3½" × 3½".

2. Lay out five four-patch units and four half-square-triangle units in three rows. Sew the units together into rows. Join the rows to make a block measuring 9½" square, including seam allowances. Make 42 blocks.

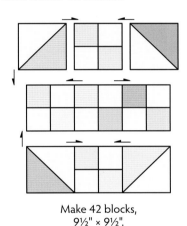

Make 42 blocks,
9½" × 9½".

ASSEMBLING THE QUILT TOP

Lay out the blocks in seven rows of six blocks each as shown in the quilt assembly diagram below. Sew the blocks together into rows. Join the rows to complete the quilt top. The quilt top should measure 54½" × 63½".

FINISHING THE QUILT

For help with any of the finishing steps, including bias binding, go to ShopMartingale.com/HowtoQuilt for free downloadable information.

1 Layer the quilt top, batting, and backing; baste.

2 Quilt by hand or machine. The quilt shown is machine quilted with an allover floral design.

3 Use the pink stripe 2¼"-wide bias strips to make the binding, and then attach the binding to the quilt.

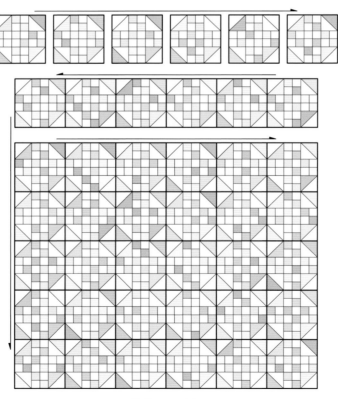

Quilt assembly

picnic

designed and pieced by LAURIE SIMPSON

 You might not be seeing stars right away as you glance at the blocks. But shooting across the quilt are no fewer than 36 eight-point stars. The trick to their subtle look? Four of the star points are prints and four are a mottled light solid. The result, a faded glory that sets the mood perfectly for a relaxing, lazy evening under the stars.

Finished quilt: **51½" × 51½"**
Finished block: **6" × 6"**

MATERIALS

Yardage is based on 42"-wide fabric and use of Cake Mix Recipe papers. Traditional cutting-method options can be found on page 95 but will require additional yardage.

 Cupcake Mix 4 (two packs)

72 squares, 5" × 5", of assorted prints in red, blue, and tan for blocks
3½ yards of white solid for blocks, setting squares, setting triangles, and binding
3¼ yards of fabric for backing
58" × 58" piece of batting

CUTTING

From the white solid, cut:
9 strips, 5" × 42"; crosscut into 72 squares, 5" × 5"
5 strips, 6½" × 42"; crosscut into 25 squares, 6½" × 6½"
2 strips, 9¾" × 42"; crosscut into:
  • 5 squares, 9¾" × 9¾"; cut the squares into quarters diagonally to yield 20 side triangles
  • 2 squares, 5⅛" × 5⅛"; cut the squares in half diagonally to yield 4 corner triangles
6 strips, 2¼" × 42"

MAKING THE UNITS

This quilt uses Cupcake Mix 4, which yields four half-square-triangle units, 1½" × 1½" finished, and four squares, 1½" × 1½" finished, per recipe paper. (You'll need 72 papers.) Press the seam allowances as indicated by the arrows.

1 Place a white 5" square on top of each assorted print square, right sides together. Pin a Cupcake Mix recipe paper to the top of each pair. Stitch on the dotted lines as indicated on the paper.

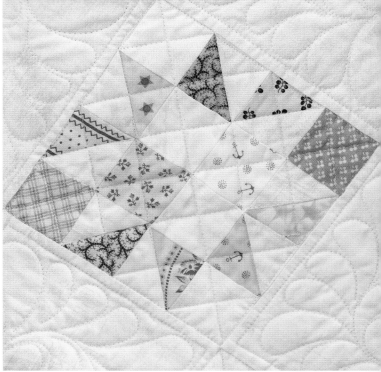

2 Cut apart the stitched squares on the solid lines. Press and remove the papers to make four half-square-triangle units measuring 2" square, including seam allowances, and four 2" squares. Make 288 units. You'll have 144 print squares and 144 white squares for making the blocks.

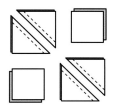

Make 288 units, 2" × 2".   Make 144 of each unit, 2" × 2".

MAKING THE BLOCKS

Lay out eight assorted half-square-triangle units, four assorted print 2" squares, and four white 2" squares in four rows of four. Sew the pieces together into rows. Join the rows to make a block measuring 6½" square, including seam allowances. Make 36 blocks.

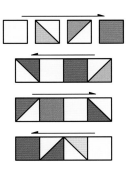 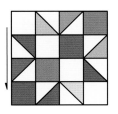

Make 36 blocks, 6½" × 6½".

Quilted by Maggi Honeyman

Laurie used Grunge fabric as the background print here. Its mottled appearance gives the slightest depth to the finished look of the quilt. Great choice!

Mix It Up!

ASSEMBLING THE QUILT TOP

Arrange the blocks and white 6½" squares in diagonal rows. Add the white side and corner triangles around the perimeter as shown in the quilt assembly diagram. Sew the pieces together into rows. Join the rows, adding the corner triangles last. The quilt top should measure 51½" square.

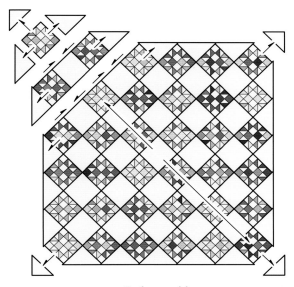

Quilt assembly

FINISHING THE QUILT

For help with any of the finishing steps, go to ShopMartingale.com/HowtoQuilt for free downloadable information.

1. Layer the quilt top, batting, and backing; baste.

2. Quilt by hand or machine. The quilt shown is machine quilted with a grid in the blocks plus a feathered wreath and outline quilting in the setting squares and triangles.

3. Use the white 2¼"-wide strips to make the binding, and then attach the binding to the quilt.

Secret Ingredients

from Laurie Simpson

We've got to hand it to her. Laurie Simpson (MinickandSimpson.blogspot.com) is well known for her stunning hand appliqué. But she can also mix it up with the best of them to showcase her signature hues in patchwork too!

Three ingredients I have to have at the ready when I'm sewing are a quilt hoop, thimble, and remote control.

My favorite mix of colors almost always includes red, white, and blue.

When a quilt design needs a little something extra, I mix in a little *more,* more piecing, more appliqué, more quilting.

One of the best mixes I buy is a special tea blend from McNulty's in New York City. It contains three different kinds of tea and is labeled as the favorite blend of longtime customer Katharine Hepburn.

If I made a mix tape, the artist whose music would be on it for sure is Ella Fitzgerald.

When it comes to mixing it up in the kitchen, two unlikely things I like to mix together are oranges and avocados.

In a bowl of snack mix, my favorites are the garlic rounds, **and my least favorites are** the mini breadsticks.

The most common mix-up I make when sewing is forgetting whether or not I've shut off the iron. I often wake up in the middle of the night and check that I've turned it off!

Stand mixer or hand mixer? Stand mixer: a wedding present that's still going strong!

churn it up

designed by ME AND MY SISTER DESIGNS

Double the size of your quilt in half the time by alternating pieced-block rows with sashing rows. Charming little Churn Dashes march across the quilt in picture-perfect rows. Gently waving feathers quilted in the solid blue sashing rows provide a nice juxtaposition for the straight lines of the pieced rows.

Finished quilt: **38¾" × 42½"**
Finished block: **4¼" × 4¼"**

MATERIALS

Yardage is based on 42"-wide fabric and use of Cake Mix Recipe papers. Traditional cutting-method options can be found on page 95 but will require additional yardage.

■ **Cupcake Mix 3** (one pack)

36 squares, 5" × 5", of assorted prints for blocks
1 yard of white solid for blocks
⅞ yard of blue solid for sashing rows
½ yard of blue check for binding
2½ yards of fabric for backing
45" × 49" piece of batting

CUTTING

From the white solid, cut:
5 strips, 5" × 42"; crosscut into 36 squares, 5" × 5"
3 strips, 2¼" × 42"; crosscut into 36 squares,
    2¼" × 2¼"

From the blue solid, cut:
5 strips, 5½" × 42"; crosscut into 5 strips, 5½" × 38¾"

From the blue check, cut:
5 strips, 2¼" × 42"

MAKING THE UNITS

This quilt uses Cupcake Mix 3, which yields four half-square-triangle units, 1¼" × 1¼" finished, and four four-patch units, 1¼" × 1¼" finished, per recipe paper. (You'll need 36 papers.) Press the seam allowances as indicated by the arrows.

1 Place a white 5" square on top of each print square, right sides together. Use a highlighter to mark the lines you *won't* be cutting on the Cupcake recipe paper as shown. Then pin a Cupcake Mix recipe paper to the top of each pair. Stitch on the dotted lines as indicated on the paper.

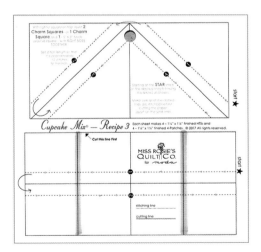

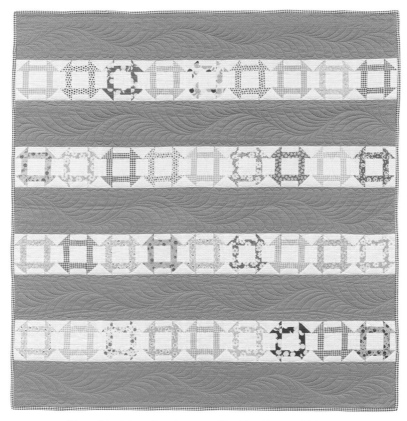

Pieced by Mary Jacobson; quilted by Sharon Elsberry

2 Cut apart the stitched squares on the solid lines, making sure to cut the pieced rectangle as shown below. Do *not* cut on the highlighted lines! Press and remove the papers to make four half-square-triangle units measuring 1¾" square, including seam allowances, and four pieced rectangles measuring 1¾" × 2¼", including seam allowances. Make 144 half-square-triangle units and 144 rail-fence units.

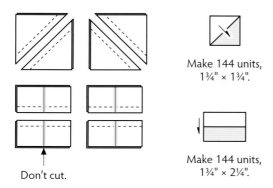

Make 144 units, 1¾" × 1¾".

Don't cut.

Make 144 units, 1¾" × 2¼".

MAKING THE BLOCKS

Using matching units from one print, lay out four half-square-triangle units, four rail-fence units, and one white 2¼" square in three rows of three. Sew the pieces together into rows. Join the rows to make a block measuring 4¾" square, including seam allowances. Make 36 blocks.

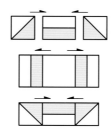

Make 36 blocks, 4¾" × 4¾".

ASSEMBLING THE QUILT TOP

1 Join nine blocks to make a row measuring 4¾" × 38¾", including seam allowances. Make four rows.

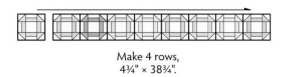

Make 4 rows,
4¾" × 38¾".

2 Lay out the block rows and blue solid strips as shown in the quilt assembly diagram. Sew the rows together to make the quilt top. The quilt top should measure 38¾" × 42½".

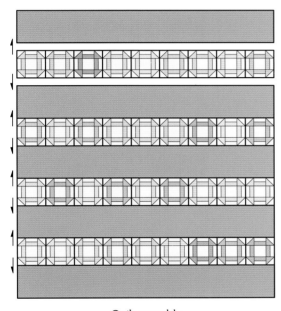

Quilt assembly

FINISHING THE QUILT

For help with any of the finishing steps, go to ShopMartingale.com/HowtoQuilt for free downloadable information.

1 Layer the quilt top, batting, and backing; baste.

2 Quilt by hand or machine. The quilt shown is machine quilted with curved lines around the Churn Dash blocks and a feather design in the blue sashing.

3 Use the blue check 2¼"-wide strips to make the binding, and then attach the binding to the quilt.

Secret Ingredients

from Barbara Groves and Mary Jacobson of Me and My Sister Designs

There'll be no fighting between you and your sister when Barbara Groves and Mary Jacobson (MeandMySisterDesigns.com) are around. Instead, you'll be laughing and sewing 'til your heart's content!

Three ingredients we have to have at the ready when we're sewing are fabric, chocolate, thread, chocolate, a sewing machine, and chocolate. (We each need three things; you figure out who needs what!)

Our favorite mix of colors almost always includes green for Barb and pink for Mary.

When a quilt design needs a little something extra, we each ask the other what she would do and then do the opposite.

One of the best mixes we buy is brownie mix.

If Barb made a mix tape, the artist whose music would be on it for sure is no one. She doesn't listen to music. She never even turns on the radio in her car. Now if you asked about TV, that would be a different and easier question!

When it comes to mixing it up in the kitchen, two unlikely things we like to mix together are ice cream and potato chips.

Two things others like to mix—but we don't—are appliqué and quilting. Our favorite is piecing.

In a bowl of snack mix, our favorite is the Chex cereal, **and our least favorites are** salty rye crisps.

The most common mix-up we make when sewing is stitching over pins and bending them.

Stand mixer or hand mixer? Hand mixer. Easier to clean up and wipe down afterward.

half and half

designed and pieced by KARLA EISENACH

If a quick quilt is on your to-do list, Karla's design uses Cake Mix 1 and you're done! Half-square triangles—big and small—are all that's needed for a borderless, I'm-mad-for-plaids throw you'll want to wrap up in right away.

Finished quilt: **64½" × 64½"**
Finished block: **8" × 8"**

MATERIALS

Yardage is based on 42"-wide fabric and use of Cake Mix Recipe papers. Traditional cutting-method options can be found on page 95 but will require additional yardage.

Cake Mix 1 (one pack)

32 squares, 10" × 10", of white solid for blocks
32 squares, 10" × 10", of assorted prints for blocks
½ yard of blue print for binding
4 yards of fabric for backing
71" × 71" piece of batting

CUTTING

From the blue print, cut:
7 strips, 2¼" × 42"

MAKING THE UNITS

This quilt uses Cake Mix 1, which yields four half-square-triangle units, 4" × 4" finished, and one half-square-triangle unit, 8" × 8" finished, per recipe paper. (You'll need 32 papers.) Press the seam allowances as indicated by the arrows.

1 Place each white square on top of a print square, right sides together. Pin a Cake Mix recipe paper to the top of each pair. Stitch on the dotted lines as indicated on the paper.

2 Cut apart the stitched squares on the solid lines, cutting the long diagonal line first. Press and remove the papers to make four A units measuring 4½" square, including seam allowances, and one B unit measuring 8½" square, including seam allowances. Make 128 of unit A and 32 of unit B.

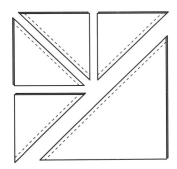

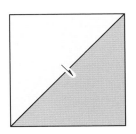

Unit A.
Make 128 units,
4½" × 4½".

Unit B.
Make 32 units,
8½" × 8½".

Quilted by Brian Clements

MAKING THE BLOCKS

Lay out four different A units in two rows of two. Sew the units together into rows. Join the rows to make a block measuring 8½" square, including seam allowances. Make 24 blocks.

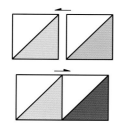

Make 24 blocks,
8½" × 8½".

ASSEMBLING THE QUILT TOP

1 Join two different A units to make a two-patch unit measuring 4½" × 8½", including seam allowances. Make 16 units.

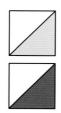

Make 16 units,
4½" × 8½".

2 Lay out the two-patch units, B units, and blocks in nine columns of eight as shown in the quilt assembly diagram. Sew the pieces together into columns. Join the columns to complete the quilt top, which should measure 64½" square.

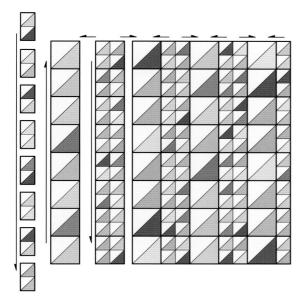

Quilt assembly

FINISHING THE QUILT

For help with any of the finishing steps, go to ShopMartingale.com/HowtoQuilt for free downloadable information.

1 Layer the quilt top, batting, and backing; baste.

2 Quilt by hand or machine. The quilt shown features an allover flower-and-leaf machine quilting design.

3 Use the blue 2¼"-wide strips to make the binding, and then attach the binding to the quilt.

Secret Ingredients

from Karla Eisenach

Sweets for the sweet! Sweetwater, that is! Karla Eisenach (TheSweetwaterCo.com) is stirring up some fun and getting the angle on accurately sewing triangles with Cake Mix papers. Here's the skinny from Karla.

My favorite mix of colors almost always includes red and cream or black and cream.

When a quilt design needs a little something extra, I love to mix in a little embroidery or personalize a block.

One of the best mixes I buy is a broccoli salad kit in the produce section.

In a bowl of snack mix, my favorites are the peanuts, **and my least favorites are** the pretzels.

The most common mix-up I make when sewing is making mistakes when writing instructions. I hate when that happens!

Stand mixer or hand mixer? I have both a stand mixer and a hand mixer. I use both, but I probably use the stand mixer more.

harbor

designed and pieced by SHERRI McCONNELL

Set on point, these stars look a bit tricky, but rest assured, there's no set-in piecing required. It'll be child's play to sew the units together using a Cupcake Mix and 5" squares. And before the sun sets, you'll have a heaping helping of twinkling stars completed!

Finished quilt: **39½" × 49½"**
Finished block: **6" × 6"**

MATERIALS

Yardage is based on 42"-wide fabric and use of Cupcake Mix Recipe papers. Traditional cutting-method options can be found on page 95 but will require additional yardage.

■ **Cupcake Mix 4** (one pack)

36 squares, 5" × 5", of assorted dark prints
    for blocks
1½ yards of beige solid for blocks, setting
    triangles, and inner border
½ yard of ecru print for sashing
⅛ yard of teal print for sashing squares
⅝ yard of navy print for outer border
½ yard of red dot for binding
2⅝ yards of fabric for backing
46" × 56" piece of batting

CUTTING

From the beige solid, cut:
5 strips, 5" × 42"; crosscut into 36 squares, 5" × 5"
1 strip, 11¼" × 42"; crosscut into 3 squares,
    11¼" × 11¼". Cut the squares into quarters
    diagonally to yield 12 side triangles (2 triangles
    are extra).
1 strip, 6⅝" × 42"; crosscut into 2 squares, 6⅝" × 6⅝".
    Cut the squares in half diagonally to yield 4 corner
    triangles.
4 strips, 1½" × 42"

From the ecru print, cut:
8 strips, 1½" × 42"; crosscut into 48 strips, 1½" × 6½"

From the teal print, cut:
2 strips, 1½" × 42"; crosscut into 31 squares,
    1½" × 1½"

From the navy print, cut:
5 strips, 3½" × 42"

From the red dot, cut:
5 strips, 2¼" × 42"

MAKING THE UNITS

This quilt uses Cupcake Mix 4, which yields four half-square-triangle units, 1½" × 1½" finished, and four squares, 1½" × 1½" finished, per recipe paper. (You'll need 36 papers.) Press the seam allowances as indicated by the arrows.

Quilted by Marion Bolt

1 Place a beige square on top of each dark square, right sides together. Pin a Cupcake Mix recipe paper to the top of each pair. Stitch on the dotted lines as indicated on the paper.

2 Cut apart the stitched squares on the solid lines. Press and remove the papers to make four half-square-triangle units measuring 2" square, including seam allowances, and four 2" squares. Make 144 units. You'll have 72 dark squares and 72 beige squares for making the blocks.

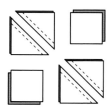

Make 144 units, 2" × 2".

Make 72 of each unit, 2" × 2".

MAKING THE BLOCKS

1 Lay out two matching half-square-triangle units, one matching dark square, and one beige square in two rows of two. Sew the pieces together into rows. Join the rows to make a quarter-block unit measuring 3½" square, including seam allowances. Make 72 units.

Make 72 units,
3½" × 3½".

2 Lay out four different quarter-block units in two rows of two, noting the orientation of the units. Sew the units together into rows. Join the rows to make a block measuring 6½" square, including seam allowances. Make 18 blocks.

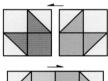
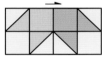
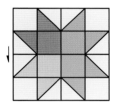

Make 18 blocks,
6½" × 6½".

ASSEMBLING THE QUILT TOP

1 Lay out the blocks, ecru 1½" × 6½" sashing strips, teal squares, beige side triangles, and beige corner triangles in diagonal rows as shown in the quilt assembly diagram. Sew the blocks and strips together into block rows. Sew the squares and strips into sashing rows. Join a sashing row to each block row to make row units; the center sashing row should remain by itself. Sew the side triangles to the ends of the row units as shown. Join the row units and remaining sashing row together, adding the corner triangles last. Trim and square up the quilt top, making sure to

leave ¼" beyond the teal squares' points for seam allowances. The quilt-top center should measure 31½" × 41½", including seam allowances.

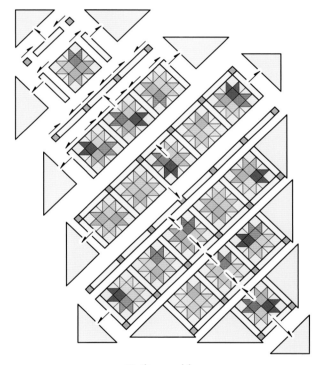

Quilt assembly

2 From the beige 1½"-wide strips, cut two 41½"-long strips and two 33½"-long strips. Sew the longer strips to opposite sides of the quilt top. Sew the shorter strips to the top and bottom of the quilt top. The quilt top should measure 33½" × 43½", including seam allowances.

Secret Ingredients

from Sherri McConnell

She's living her best life—a quilting life, that is! One of the most well-organized quilters we know, Sherri McConnell (AQuiltingLife.com) loves to share her sewing-room secrets with fellow quilters.

Three ingredients I have to have at the ready when I'm sewing are a new rotary-cutter blade, Alexa (for music), and my very own custom Peanut M&M's and almonds mix.

My favorite mix of colors almost always includes blue in any shade, from aqua to navy.

When a quilt design needs a little something extra, I love to mix in low-volume fabric.

One of the best mixes I buy is Chex Mix. I love it!

If I made a mix tape, the artist whose music would be on it for sure is Justin Timberlake.

When it comes to mixing it up in the kitchen, two unlikely things I like to mix together are ice cream and anything.

Two things others like to mix—but I don't—are purple and anything.

In a bowl of snack mix, my favorites and my least favorites are . . . hmmm. I love everything. But don't try to put corn nuts in the mix!

The most common mix-up I make when sewing? If it's late, I make a lot of mix-ups. So, I try to call it a day by 10:30 p.m.

Stand mixer or hand mixer? We have both, but I love the stand mixer best.

3 Join three navy strips end to end. From the pieced strip, cut two 43½"-long strips. Trim the remaining two strips to 39½" long. Sew the longer strips to opposite sides of the quilt top. Sew the shorter strips to the top and bottom of the quilt top. The quilt top should measure 39½" × 49½".

Adding borders

FINISHING THE QUILT

For help with any of the finishing steps, go to ShopMartingale.com/HowtoQuilt for free downloadable information.

1 Layer the quilt top, batting, and backing; baste.

2 Quilt by hand or machine. The quilt shown is machine quilted with an allover clamshell design.

3 Use the red dot 2¼"-wide strips to make the binding, and then attach the binding to the quilt.

Patchwork Yields

FROM CAKE MIX AND CUPCAKE MIX PAPERS

All of the Cake Mix and Cupcake Mix recipe papers are designed to be easy to use for creating precise patchwork units. Each one yields a different mix of half-square-triangle, quarter-square-triangle, four-patch, and/or rail fence units in different sizes. Each project in the book lists exactly which package of recipe papers you need to make the quilt shown. However, if you don't have the recipe cards or don't wish to sew on paper (what?!), you can make substitutions by cutting and sewing the number and sizes of units listed for each block in the pattern you are making.

Cake Mix	Number of units	Finished size of units	Cut size of squares and rectangles	Trimmed size of half-square-triangle units
1	4	4" half-square-triangle units	5" × 5"	4½" square
	1	8" half-square-triangle unit	9" × 9"	8½" square
2	10	2¼" half-square-triangle units	3¼" × 3¼"	2¾" square
	2	4½" half-square-triangle units	5½" × 5½"	5" square
3	18	2" half-square-triangle units	3" × 3"	2½" square
4	8	3¾" or 4" half-square-triangle units	4¾" × 4¾" or 5" × 5"	4¼" square or 4½" square
5	4	3½" half-square-triangle units	4½" × 4½"	4" square
	4	3½" four-patch units	2¼" × 2¼"	N/A
6	8	2" half-square-triangle units	3" × 3"	2½" square
	8	2" rail-fence units	1½" × 2½"	N/A
	2	2" squares	2½" × 2½"	N/A
7	4	3" half-square-triangle units	4" × 4"	3½" square
	16	1½" half-square-triangle units	2½" × 2½"	2" square
8	4	3" half-square-triangle units	4" × 4"	3½" square
	30	1" half-square-triangle units	2" × 2"	1½" square
9	4	3" quarter-square-triangle units	4¼" × 4¼"	3½" square
	8	1½" half-square-triangle units	2½" × 2½"	2" square
	8	2" squares	2½" × 2½"	N/A
10	4	3" half-square-triangle units	4" × 4"	3½" square
	5	3" four-patch units	2" × 2"	N/A
	1	4½" half-square-triangle unit	5½" × 5½"	5" square
11	16	1½" half-square-triangle units	2½" × 2½"	2" square
	2	2" squares	2½" × 2½"	N/A
12	4	3¾" half-square-triangle units	4¾" × 4¾"	4¼" square
	4	3¾" four-patch units	2⅜" × 2⅜"	N/A
	2	1⅞" squares	2⅜" × 2⅜"	N/A

Cake Mix Yields

Cupcake Mix Yields

Cupcake Mix	Number of units	Finished size of units	Cut size of squares and rectangles	Trimmed size of half-square-triangle units
1	1	3" half-square-triangle unit	4" × 4"	3½" square
	4	1½" half-square-triangle units	2½" × 2½"	2" square
2	8	1½" or 1¼" half-square-triangle units	2½" × 2½" or 2¼" × 2¼"	2" square or 1¾" square
3	4	1¼" half-square-triangle unit	2¼" × 2¼"	1¾" square
	4	1¼" four-patch units	1¾" × 1¾"	N/A
4	4	1½" half-square-triangle units	2½" × 2½"	2" square
	4	1½" squares	2" × 2"	N/A